*Prayer
and
Personal
Religion*

by
John B. Coburn

LAYMAN'S
THEOLOGICAL
LIBRARY

THE WESTMINSTER PRESS

PHILADELPHIA

Acknowledgment:
  In the preparation of this book I am grateful for the encourage-
ment of the Rev. Alan G. Whittemore, O.H.C., who over the
years has been for me, as for many, a symbol of the meaning of
the life of prayer and personal religion. He has read parts of the
original draft of the manuscript; the illustration from William
James in Chapter 4 and the form of meditation in Chapter 5
are his.

J. B. C.

Library of Congress Catalog Card No.: 57-5397

PRINTED IN THE UNITED STATES OF AMERICA

16 17 18 19 20

CONTENTS

FOREWORD

The religious book market is full of books for "the intelligent layman." Some are an insult to his intelligence. Others are covertly written for professional theologians. A few are genuine helps in communicating the faith.

In this spate of books being thrust at the lay reader, what distinctive place can the Layman's Theological Library claim to hold? For one thing, it will try to remind the layman that he *is* a theologian. The close conjunction of the words "layman" and "theological" in the title of the series is not by chance but by design. For theology is not an irrelevant pastime of seminary professors. It is the occupation of every Christian, the moment he begins to think about, or talk about, or communicate, his Christian faith. The injunction to love God *with all his mind* necessarily involves the layman in theology. He can never avoid theology; if he refuses to think through his faith, he simply settles for inferior theology.

Furthermore, the Layman's Theological Library will attempt to give a *wholeness* in its presentation of the Christian faith. Its twelve volumes cover the main areas of Christian faith and practice. They are written out of similar convictions which the authors share about the uniqueness of the Christian faith. All the authors are convinced that Christian faith can be made relevant, that it can be made understandable without becoming innocuous, and that (particularly in view of the current "return to religion") it is crucially important for the layman to commit himself to more than "religion in general."

7

The Layman's Theological Library, then, will attempt a fresh exploration of the Christian faith, and what it can mean in the life of twentieth century man.

Probably the most baffling aspect of the Christian faith is the one under discussion in this volume. A great many people these days can see some relevance in the analysis which the Christian faith makes of our human situation. We have seen so many false gods totter and fall, that the Christian appraisal is one that we are more willing than heretofore to entertain seriously.

But there is a wide gap between an " analysis of our situation " and a living relationship with the living God himself. It is to help in bridging this difficult gap that the present volume has been written. The author does not presuppose that we have made vast strides in the spiritual life. He starts with us right where we are, in the midst of our confusions, perplexities, and discouragements. And he takes us step by step into what is for most of us the relatively unknown land of prayer, so that we can come not only to know *about* God, but to *know* God and love him — and not only that, but more important, to see that we are known *of* God and loved by him.

Prayer for many is like a foreign land. When we go there, we go as tourists. Like most tourists, we feel uncomfortable and out of place. Like most tourists, we therefore move on before too long and go somewhere else. So this book is a kind of map or guidebook to the foreign land of prayer. All else that needs to be said about it is that it has been written, not by a tourist, but by a native of that significant soil.

ROBERT McAFEE BROWN

PRAYER IS RESPONSE TO GOD

The purpose of this volume in the Layman's Theological Library is to help people to pray and to grow in their personal religious life. It is, therefore, a book about their inner life and their personal relationship with God. Although this relationship is always unique for each person, there is nevertheless a general way by which God deals with men and through which they respond. This book is concerned with this general pattern. It is written with the hope, however, that each person who reads it will be helped to understand how God is already dealing with him personally, and therefore to respond more fully to him. This is the way by which most of us come finally to discover that it is God himself who teaches us best to pray.

Prayer is response to God. The first step is God's. He begins the relationship with us. When we pray, we have made our response.

If you have ever prayed, you have already responded to God. Indeed, if you have even *wanted* to pray, you have responded. In either case it is a sure sign that God has already touched you. And if you have never prayed, it may be because you have not recognized his touch.

Look for a moment at some of the ways God touches people. You may recognize some of these experiences as your own.

God may already have done more in your life than you suspect.

Have you ever, for example, had the experience of standing outdoors at night alone, looking up into the heavens? It is a brilliantly clear night and the stars stand out so distinctly that you feel as though you could almost reach up and touch one. As you look at this canopy above you, you are suddenly overwhelmed by a sense of the immensity and greatness and mysterious order in the universe, and with a sense of your own tiny insignificance in contrast. If you have ever had such an experience, both exalting you and humbling you at the same time, God may have touched you, for this is one of the ways God breaks in on people.

A somewhat similar experience is described by a young college graduate. "In recent years," he writes, "I have been struck more and more by my inability to direct my life according to my own best intentions. I find myself again and again caught in patterns of behavior I had firmly resolved to avoid. I discover a weakness within myself which I had not been aware of. At the same time, when I go off on long walks in the country, which has always been a pleasure of mine, I have a vague, uneasy sense that something else or someone else is around, and trying to communicate with me. So, I ask, ' What goes on here? ' " If you have ever felt yourself confronted by some such sense of " otherness," which is frequently mysterious and awesome and perhaps even frightening, you have been exposed to one of the experiences by which God breaks through to a person's consciousness.

Some people recognize God first simply through a sense of duty. One man, attempting to explain how he responded to life after he had in a few months lost his wife and two of his children, said: " At that time I soon discovered life was spelling out for me a four letter word, d-u-t-y. So I have tried ever since to do my duty to my colleagues, my family, and my community." It was through this that he came gradually to relate these duties to his God. So wherever there is an "ought" in your life, when you are faced with nothing to go on except what you know is "right," there is one of the ways God's touch is seen.

Again, if you have ever had the suspicion that the only problem you really have is yourself — and not somebody or something else — then you may have an undercurrent in your life of feeling guilty. Perhaps you have had no clear idea just what it was you were guilty of, nor by whom judged, but there has been a persistent gnawing, uneasy feeling. This is sometimes an opening into your life that God is responsible for, through which you can turn to him.

To take an entirely different kind of experience, you may at one time or another have been taken quite out of yourself and "transported into another world." This sometimes happens when people are confronted by sheer beauty — a sunset or a work of art or a beautiful woman — or when they are "carried away" by great music, or become "lost" in contemplating a manificent idea. Men and women are "inspired" to become more than they normally are when they come face to face with saints, or indeed when they fall in love. There is frequently given a sense of yearning or longing for something the world cannot give. These experiences may come from God, so if you have ever had any such "inspiration" you may have been touched, however lightly, by him.

Perhaps the most obvious "religious" way by which men have been drawn toward God has been through the persistent appeal of the Bible and the church. Even among those who have turned away from organized religion there has been a kind of inner restlessness which has caused them to take an almost wistful look at the Christian faith. So they turn from time to time to that which represents God. They read the Bible, perhaps off and on for years; or infrequently they attend services of the church. You may have known this peculiar and hard to define fascination, either of the Bible or the church, and been drawn by one of the ways God often uses to touch men.

These, then, are some of the human experiences through which God breaks into the lives of men. If you have ever had any like them, and because of them have prayed, or even wanted to pray, you have been touched by God and responded to him. You may not have known it then. You may have difficulty believing it now. But this is the starting place: prayer is response to God. Prayer is always the second step in response to the initiative taken by God.

We need now to get some accurate picture of this God to whom we respond. When you think of God, how do you picture him — as a policeman, or a judge, or a kindly old grandfather, or a remote First Cause? These are common ideas of God, and they are wrong. These false ideas of God are responsible for most of the trouble people have in life. If you begin with the wrong idea of God, then you get the wrong idea of yourself and of other people and of the relation of God to them. Then, with the wrong idea of everyone, you are in trouble.

Here is another picture of God. It is not entirely accurate, of course, because man's words can never describe him perfectly. It is a rough picture, and a simple one, and it is only approximately true, but it fits within a Christian framework. Try to think of God in some such way as this. It may take some believing at the outset. Remember, however, that you can never get in trouble by thinking thoughts of God that are too great.

God is a Person. He is infinitely more than this, but he is at least this. And this is the place to begin, for if you think of God primarily as a person, then when you speak to him you can say, " You," and, " I." When he addresses you, he in turn speaks to a person and also says, " you." Thus a two-way personal conversation, set in a personal relationship, can be set up. This personal conversation is the essence of prayer.

God is a Person who thinks and acts. His thoughts and actions are perfect. He always "does the truth"; his works are without fail beautiful and good; and he is responsible for joy and peace in the hearts of men. His actions in and through people and nature always have such characteristics as these.

Best of all, however, God is a *loving* Person. The reason he began the world and created everything within it is because of his love. He loves everybody everywhere all the time. Indeed he created *you* because he loves you. You can actually think of him best as one who loves you as though you were the only person in the world. This is how much he loves you. Now what he wants above all else is to have you love him in return. You know from your own experience with human love that this is what a lover always wants: to have the person he loves respond to him with love.

So God has been trying in and through all the experiences of your life so to touch you that you will begin to turn to him and end by loving him. He has been striving to break through not only in the out-of-the-ordinary experiences mentioned above, but in all the events and relationships of your life, whether they be of love and peace, sorrow and death, guilt and sin, or beauty and joy. *There is no experience that has not been a means by which God has been trying to communicate with you.* He has been doing everything he possibly can to overcome the separation between you and him. As we shall see later, he will stop at nothing that is not contrary to his nature — not even the death of his Son — so that you and he may be brought together to converse with each other, saying, " I," and " you," that you may know God as your lover and yourself as his beloved.

If you can get this kind of picture of God, or anything like this, you have enough to start with intelligently. There are experiences in your life that can best be understood as experiences through which God has been trying to touch you. They begin to make sense because now, perhaps for the first time, you can see how God is involved in them. Through them he has found you. Indeed, you would not have read to this page in the book if he had not already found you.

You may conclude this chapter with an experiment by which you can see for yourself the truth of what God has already done in your life. The experiment has two steps:

1. Take this present moment and ask yourself: " What are the good things I have in my life right now for which I know I am not responsible? " Make a list: your life itself, someone who loves you and trusts you, your intelligence, your parents and family background, work to do, friends . . . what else? Make your list. Now test this statement:

Everything good in your life that you know you are not responsible for, God is responsible for.

2. Next, write down all the things in your life at this moment that you consider evil. What are they? Sickness, failures, death of loved ones, misunderstandings, hopes broken, your sins (do not slide over these — be specific) . . . what else? Make your list. Now test this statement:

Everything in your life that you consider evil, God permits.

What are your findings? Can you point to any good in your life that you believe God is responsible for? Can you see any evil in your life that is permitted by God for a special purpose? If your answer to either question is " Yes," then that is precisely where God is touching you now. It is from this place that you can turn to him in response to his initiative. This is the beginning of a personal relationship which is started by God and which continues as you increasingly come to know and love and serve him.

Your prayer is your response. It is the second step. The first step was God's. It has already been taken.

The way to begin is to say at this moment, "O God, *you* . . ." Once you have said "God, *you*" and not "God, *he,*" you have begun to pray. This is your response to God. Prayer is always response to God. It is a second step you can take now.

"O God, I have this . . . to say to *you.*"
"What have you to say to *me* . . . ?"

2

BE YOURSELF AND BEGIN WHERE YOU ARE

It is a strange thing about God, but he does not mind being last choice. We do not like even to be second choice, whether it is to play on a sand-lot baseball team or to be a guest at dinner. God, however, is content to be last choice.

This chapter is for people who make God their last choice. If you have tried other ways of life apart from God and found them wanting, then this chapter is for you. Let us suppose you have made the experiment at the end of the previous chapter and now decide to respond to God. There are two simple rules to follow at the beginning. The first one is: *Be yourself.*

Be natural before God. Do not pretend to be what you are not. Do not pretend to emotions you do not feel. Tell him whatever is on your heart and mind with whatever words are most natural to you. You do not have to speak to him in " religious " language about " spiritual " matters only. If it is easier to say " you know " than " thou knowest," say it. We shall see later how the great prayers of the ages, clothed in prayer form and with their majestic language, can quite properly be used. But when you begin, speak as naturally and as easily as you would to a friend, since God is just that. Be yourself.

This matter of being yourself, however, goes deeper than language. It goes to the depths of your feelings about God and the circumstances of your life. You do not have to feel " pious " before God, or "holy" or "spiritual." You are meant to be honest. Do not, therefore, try to hide your true feelings from God. If you feel resentful before God, because someone you love has died, do not say with your lips, "O God thy will be done," when underneath in your heart you are saying: "This is a terrible thing you have done. What an awful God you are!" This dishonesty will set up smoldering resentment within, and it will break out destructively sooner or later.

The important thing is to tell God exactly how you do feel: "O God, I hate you for this! How can you be so unjust, so heartless! If this is what you are really like, I'm through with you before we begin."

You cannot cover up before God. Be honest and natural and express yourself just as you are — not as you imagine God (or somebody else) says you ought to be. *This natural expression of yourself at the outset is the guarantee that you can go on to a creative, free, and mature relationship with God.* Be yourself.

A young father sat grim-faced throughout the funeral service of his four-year-old son who had died of polio. As he listened to the opening words, "I know that my Redeemer liveth," he kept murmuring under his breath: "God, I'll get back at you for this. I'll get back at you for this."

This was the first honest conversation he had ever had with God.

Later he commented: "That was a foolish thing to say, I suppose. How could I ever get back at God? Yet it was honest and it kept the relationship with God open. That was the way I felt, and it was right to clear the atmosphere and get it all off my chest. For then I gradually came to myself and saw that death does have to go into some final framework and only God can absorb it. I read and reread all those experiences of men suffering before God, especially Job, and in time his sentiments became mine, or almost mine. I know now that my Redeemer *does* live. And I don't think I should know it, deep down inside, if I hadn't been mad at my Redeemer once — and said so."

Be yourself. Do not pretend. It is the only honest, open way to God. Anyhow, to try to hide anything from God is a sheer waste of time. He already knows everything that is in your heart. In the words of an ancient prayer, he is the God " unto whom all hearts are open, all desires known, and from whom no secrets are hid." And this means *your* heart, *your* desires and *your* secrets. So be yourself.

The second rule is this: *Begin where you are.* So far as your beginning prayer is concerned you are where your needs are. Look for a moment at those needs. What do you think you now need most in order to have a completely fulfilled life? If you are like most people, you will begin to pray because you need:

peace of mind
power for living
to be forgiven.

Let us take a brief look at each of these. You may want *peace of mind* so that you can accept life. Your need is to be able to take all that life does to you. You search for an inner composure and calm that will give you a basic stability when the storms blow and sickness, sufferings, sorrow, defeats, and failures descend. Especially may you long for a peace within that overcomes all fears and anxieties.

This search for peace of mind seldom has anything to do with material needs or wants. Frequently it is the most prosperous outwardly who are the most fearful inwardly. A relatively young insurance man, by common consent the most successful agent in one of the western regions of the country, in a burst of confidence, described himself in these words: " I am a fear-ridden man. I am afraid I shall be an utter failure. I fear I shall get no prospects; when I do, I'm afraid I shall lose them. Once they are signed, I'm afraid they won't pass their physical examinations, or pay their premiums. No big fears. I'm just riddled with little fears." And he concluded: " If anybody ever needed religion, believe me, I'm the fellow. Nobody else seems to be able to help me; maybe God can."

You may be one of those, then, who turn to God out of your need for peace of mind. If you are, begin by telling him of your need and asking frankly and deliberately for help.

Or, you may be looking for *power for living*. Your life seems to have gone along so far and then you have run out of gas. The tasks of creative living seem too great for you. The demands are too much. The ball goes over the plate too fast. Some will say, " I can't seem to get my feet off the ground," and others, " I always seem to be up in the air." And they both mean the same thing: the sense of purposefulness in life is gone; there is no power.

This is the problem of middle age more than any other. The satisfactions of physical sensations have begun to dwindle. You begin now to realize that your mental powers are not going to solve all the problems of human existence. The enthusiasm of emotional loyalties begins to diminish. You have long since compromised earlier ideals, and youthful hopes have been broken. You begin to settle down to mediocrity and life "as it really is."

Boredom sets in, coupled with a curious sense of restlessness. You may one day find yourself on a treadmill, and realize that you have been there for a long time. This is the stage of too much rushing for commuters' trains, and too many harried business conferences; too many lost golf balls, and too many Martinis; too much television (*anything* to relieve the boredom) and too many divorces. The middle-aged kick over the traces in hopes of finding new kicks in life.

And it all reveals a sound instinct which declares: " Surely there is more to life than this! Certainly this isn't all there is to it! " For underneath all these surface phenomena there is an inner urge to have your life count, to be able to direct it intelligently for some creative purpose, and to clothe it with dignity and meaning. So, if there is no place else to go, no one else to turn to, you turn to God to give you power for living. If this is your need, turn and ask him for help.

If it is not peace of mind you need, nor power for living, then you probably know your need above all other needs — *to be forgiven.* As a matter of fact, there are no neat three-way divisions here, and nearly all of us belong in varying degrees in all three groups. The most basic need, however, intimately bound up with the other two, is this: to be made clean.

As you look back over the years, you can see what has gradually happened. Perhaps at first there was nothing more than the exciting adventures of doing wrong to see how much you could get away with. Then came all the foolish, reckless acts of youth and the indulgences of the flesh. More dangerous was the casual compromise with truth and the occasional deliberate lie to protect yourself. And all along there have been outbursts of temper, or petty acts of selfishness. Worst of all, you remember hurting the people you love most, and turning your back on so many opportunities to show them your love. And now it has all added up to a condition where most of the time you are primarily concerned about yourself, think more highly of yourself than you know you ought to think, don't give much consideration to anyone beyond your own immediate circle, and sometimes not even beyond yourself.

You can fill in the details. They all add up to a great burden of guilt. And it is this weight more than any other burden in life which slows you down and robs you of peace of mind and power for living. This is the burden from which you need to be freed. And since no psychiatrist, nor any other human being, can relieve you of it, God will. He will forgive you and make you clean — if you turn to him and ask him.

When we are dealing with our need for forgiveness we are close to the very heart of all religion, and especially the Christian religion. The simple fact stated bluntly is this: we all are in difficulty in life because we are separated from God. That separation is our sin. Once we confess our sin, God takes it away, and then we are right with him. Once we have been made clean, *then* we are given also the keys to peace of mind and power for living.

So, then, these are the needs that people have — for peace of mind, power for living, to be forgiven. When you think you know what your need is, that is when you begin to pray. Do not worry about its being a " selfish " need. It may very well be. But if you know it, God knows it. Your beginning prayers can properly be " selfish " prayers. These are the initial lines of communication with God, and as such are of crucial importance. They will change their character as your prayer continues and time goes on. There is nothing " wrong " with them, any more than there is something " wrong " with the toddling steps of a small child. You begin where you are. Then you move on with firmer steps as you grow into manhood.

The First Three Prayers

So then you begin. God is your choice. You have responded and begun to pray. Begin very simply — and briefly — the first few days, even weeks. The simpler, the better. Simple and direct prayers, at this juncture, will help to keep *you* simple and direct. Long, complicated prayers at this juncture will only cause confusion; they should be avoided like the plague.

There are three prayers at the beginning. The first two will probably come quite naturally. The first is, " *O God, help me,*" or, "Help someone I love." The key here is to be specific, simple, and direct. "Help me to . . . get better . . . control my temper . . . find a job . . . meet this test . . . keep calm inside . . . or whatever . . . help me. Or, this person . . ."

The second is, *"O God, forgive me."* The key here is the same — be specific, simple, and direct. "O God, I am sorry I spoke in anger . . . did not speak in courage . . . was jealous . . . drank too much the night before last . . . was impatient with the children . . . gossiped about the boss . . . kicked the dog . . . whatever . . . forgive me."

These are the two obvious first steps in prayer, and the third, though less obvious to begin with, is in the long run even more important. It is, *"O God, thank you."* Here attention begins to be withdrawn from yourself and to be directed toward God. The key is the same — be specific, simple, and direct. "O God, thank you for . . . my wife . . . my life . . . my health . . . my job . . . my brains . . . my friend John . . . whatever . . . thank you."

So then the preliminaries are over. Now we can proceed directly. This is where you are, so: *Be yourself and begin where you are.* And remember: *This is where God has brought you.*

You can do no better now than say:
    "O God, help me . . ."
        "Forgive me for . . ."
            "Thank you for . . ."

3

CLEARING THE GROUND

The foundation stones of prayer are the prayers you say. The base upon which the life of prayer is built is simply "saying your prayers"—regularly, devotedly, and intelligently. This is the support upon which all further prayer rests. So it is important to get the foundation secure. To use the figure of constructing a house, this chapter will be devoted to clearing the ground for the foundation stones. The preliminary matters to be dealt with are three.

When to Pray

It does not make any difference what time you take. Take any time. But, once having taken it, stick to it.

There are many pressures on your time. All kinds of important matters crowd in and make demands. If you do not give God the time he demands, you will become so involved that you will not have any time left to give him. So take time — any time — and keep it.

Some people pray best early in the morning, before they are involved in all the events of the day; others pray best at night, when the world has quieted down. Some pray on subways and buses, others during their lunch hours, and some on their way home from work.

There is no rule, but obviously the best time for quiet (and quiet is your best companion for conversation with God) is in the morning when you can offer him the events of the day that stretch before, and in the evening when in his presence you can review those events, and so commend them and yourself to God for the night.

The morning is quiet because you have not become involved in the day and are fresh; nighttime is good because you can open the levels of your consciousness to God for him to dwell there as you sleep. But do not leave all your prayer to the end of the day — else, tired, you fall asleep before prayer is done. Morning is the time for work in prayer, the evening for rest in prayer.

Where to Pray

The basic principle here is the same: pray anywhere you want to, but, having chosen a place, make it your habitual place of prayer. Jesus recommended a closet. If you have a big enough one, you need look no farther. If you do not, find a place that has the virtue of closets: privacy. Your need is to be alone with God, where you say what you want to, in any way you want to, and where you will be neither overheard nor interrupted. The need for a familiar, secluded place of retreat for your private, daily, personal prayer cannot be overemphasized.

It can obviously be a place in your home. It could be as simple a place as your armchair. You may have a favorite religious picture or cross on the wall in front of you, and the devotional books you have found most helpful beside you. The other natural place for private prayer is in a church. Perhaps you can stop in during the day, either going to or coming from work. This is a house of prayer which already provides a devotional atmosphere, not only because of its architecture, but because of the prayers of faithful people offered there over the years. You can meet God most easily if you go to meet him in his house.

In any case, select a place of privacy and day by day go there to talk with God. Your prayers and his presence will soon make it a holy place.

How to Pray

One distinguished clergyman reports that he can pray best when he is lying on the sand at the shore. A professor of religion writes that he prays best when he has a pipe in his mouth and his feet on his desk. Ignatius of Loyola recommends standing to say the Lord's Prayer and then advancing one step to kneel and continue one's prayers. " If kneeling," he writes, " I find that which I desire, I will not change to another position."

The point is: in private prayer you can pray standing, sitting, kneeling, or lying down. Use whatever position is most convenient to you. The only rule is to be as natural as you can. You may find help, however, in the traditional customs of standing for thanksgiving and adoration, kneeling for confession and intercession, and sitting for meditation.

The words spoken should be simple and direct. They should be *your* words. Your words will make the prayers *your* prayers, and your prayers will make it a direct, personal conversation between you and God. So speak as naturally and easily as you would to a friend. Use the words that rise most simply to your lips. And let your prayers at the beginning revolve around the three points we discussed in the last chapter: " God . . . please help . . . I am sorry . . . I thank you."

You will find shortly that you need help in your prayers. You will say sooner or later all you think you have to say. You will become repetitious, and you will be afraid you are getting bogged down.

This is the time to turn to the prayers of others for help. You may use little modern devotional pamphlets or books. One of the most helpful current books is John Baillie's *A Diary of Private Prayer*. An unusual collection of prayers of the ages is *Uncommon Prayers,* by Cecil Hunt. *Prayers Old and New,* issued by the Forward Movement, includes prayers for every need and concern. In addition, nearly every denomination publishes its own special devotional material.

Whatever you do, to whatever source you turn, do this: *Make these prayers your own.* Do not just read them, but take them and remake them so that, as they give you material and direction, they become yours.

Here, for example, is a traditional prayer, based originally on some words of the Old Testament prophet Isaiah, which has become a familiar prayer in Christian public worship: " O God of peace, who hast taught us that in returning and rest we shall be saved, in quietness and in confidence shall be our strength: By the might of thy Spirit lift us, we pray Thee, to Thy presence, where we may be still and know that Thou art God; through Jesus Christ our Lord."

Now make this your own by saying *slowly:* " O God of peace, who has taught *me* that in returning and rest *I* shall be saved, in quietness and in confidence shall be *my* strength: By the might of thy Spirit lift *me, I* pray thee, to thy presence, where *I* may be still and know that thou art God; through Jesus Christ *my* Lord."

We should underline one especially rich source of material for private personal prayers: The Psalms. These are prayers offered to God when a man is angry, when he is happy, when he is guilty and sensual, when he is thankful and trusting, when he is suspicious and full of despair, when he is in love and filled with adoration.

These are wonderful prayers to make your own. There is a supply here you never can exhaust, and to become familiar with some few of them will greatly strengthen, deepen, and enrich your own prayers. Listen to just a few. That is, listen to yourself as you read them aloud slowly, making them your own.

PRAISE

" *Bless the Lord, O my soul:* and all that is within me, bless his holy name.

Bless the Lord, O my soul, and forget not all his benefits " (Ps. 103:1, 2).

" *I will sing unto the Lord* as long as I live: I will sing praise to my God while I have my being " (Ps. 104:33).

" *Thou art my God,* and I will praise thee: thou art my God, I will exalt thee.

O give thanks unto the Lord; for he is good: for his mercy endureth for ever " (Ps. 118:28, 29).

CONFESSION

" *Have mercy upon me, O God,* according to thy loving-kindness; according unto the multitude of thy tender mercies blot out my transgressions.

Wash me thoroughly from mine iniquity, and cleanse me from my sin.

For I acknowledge my transgressions: and my sin is ever before me.

Against thee, thee only, have I sinned, and done this evil in thy sight. . . .

Hide thy face from my sins, and blot out all mine iniquities.

Create in me a clean heart, O God; and renew a right spirit within me.

Cast me not away from thy presence; and take not thy Holy Spirit from me.

Restore unto me the joy of thy salvation; and uphold me with thy free Spirit. . . .

The sacrifices of God are a broken spirit: a broken and a contrite heart, O God, thou wilt not despise " (Ps. 51:1-4, 9-12, 17).

HELP

" *Hear my prayer, O Lord,* and let my cry come unto thee.

Hide not thy face from me in the day when I am in trouble; incline thine ear unto me: in the day when I call answer me speedily " (Ps. 102:1, 2).

" *In thee, O Lord, do I put my trust;* let me never be ashamed: deliver me in thy righteousness.

Bow down thine ear to me; deliver me speedily: be thou my strong rock, for a house of defense to save me.

For thou art my rock and my fortress; therefore for thy name's sake lead me, and guide me.

Pull me out of the net that they have laid privily for me: for thou art my strength.

Into thine hand I commit my spirit: thou hast redeemed me, O Lord God of truth " (Ps. 31:1-5).

" *Out of the depths have I cried unto thee,* O Lord.

Lord, hear my voice: let thine ears be attentive to the voice of my supplications.

If thou, Lord, shouldest mark iniquities, O Lord, who shall stand?

But there is forgiveness with thee, that thou mayest be feared.

I wait for the Lord, my soul doth wait, and in his word do I hope.

My soul waiteth for the Lord more than they that watch for the morning: I say, more than they that watch for the morning.

Let Israel hope in the Lord: for with the Lord there is mercy, and with him is plenteous redemption.

And he shall redeem Israel from all his iniquities " (Ps. 130).

CONFIDENCE

" *He that dwelleth* in the secret place of the Most High shall abide under the shadow of the Almighty.

I will say of the Lord, He is my refuge and my fortress: my God; in him will I trust.

Surely he shall deliver thee from the snare of the fowler, and from the noisome pestilence.

He shall cover thee with his feathers, and under his wings shalt thou trust: his truth shall be thy shield and buckler.

Thou shalt not be afraid for the terror by night; nor for the arrow that flieth by day;

Nor for the pestilence that walketh in darkness; nor for the destruction that wasteth at noonday.

A thousand shall fall at thy side, and ten thousand at thy right hand; but it shall not come nigh thee " (Ps. 91:1-7).

" *The Lord is my shepherd;* I shall not want.

He maketh me to lie down in green pastures: he leadeth me beside the still waters.

He restoreth my soul: he leadeth me in the paths of righteousness for his name's sake.

Yea, though I walk through the valley of the shadow of death, I will fear no evil: for thou art with me; thy rod and thy staff they comfort me.

Thou preparest a table before me in the presence of mine enemies: thou anointest my head with oil; my cup runneth over.

Surely goodness and mercy shall follow me all the days of my life: and I will dwell in the house of the Lord for ever " (Ps. 23).

Such prayers as these become your prayers when you make them your own. This you can do as you slowly and deliberately translate the words of the psalmists into your own words. Thus you are helped to express and direct through every mood and experience of your own the movement of your heart toward God. This is personal prayer.

So much, then, for the clearing of the ground. This begins with the regular saying of your prayers, as often as possible in the same place. Use your own words as naturally as you can. When you need help, turn to the prayers of others and make them your own. This is to prepare the way for the laying of the foundations.

4

THE FOUNDATION STONES OF PRAYER

Having cleared the ground for the laying of the foundation, let us look more closely at the foundation stones themselves. There are five basic kinds of prayer. Like all good foundations, they are for the most part hidden from sight. As you quietly put these stones in place by regularly "saying your prayers" you make it possible later to build the proper structure for your soul.

The Prayer of Adoration

To adore God is to say, "God, I love you." It is the most important single prayer we can ever offer him.

Your immediate reaction may be: "But I can't honestly say I love God. I'm not even sure I like him. Besides, I've only just begun to know him."

To which one can only reply: Don't worry about this. You don't have to love him when you begin. Very few people do — just as few couples fall in love at first sight. But if you pay enough attention to God, you will come in time to love him, because he is lovable; indeed, he is Love. He will help you to love him. The point here is simply that at the very center of your relationship with God is this act of your will to love. It is this which brings richness and strength to your prayers and thus to yourself. To adore God is prayer's central act.

To ask *why* one should adore God is like asking a lover why he adores his beloved. His only answer can be, " Why, because she *is*." So a man loves God, not because he has helped him or answered his prayers or forgiven him his sin, or for any gifts he has given. He loves God simply because God is God and he is a man related to him. The prayer of adoration is to thank God for God!

God, as we saw in our opening chapter, is a Person with perfect intelligence and will who is perfect Love. We can think of him best, then, as the source of all love. All the fragmentary bits of loveliness and holiness that we know come from him, and are all gathered up in him.

In his heart there wells up a constant flow of love, which is poured out upon his creation in holiness and beauty. Only because of his love did he once create and does he now sustain the world. For those who see with the eyes of faith the whole world shows forth his glory: from the bursting forth of buds in the beauty of springtime to the love that causes a man to lay down his life for a friend. All life is surrounded and supported by God's perfect love around us and above us, beneath us and within us. We live and move and have our being within him. He is the beginning and the ending of our life and all lives forever. He is the be-all and end-all from everlasting to everlasting. That which is eternal is God and his holiness and beauty and love with which he surrounds us.

The prayer of adoration, before such grandeur, is a simple and holy one: " I love you."

The only helpful analogy, and even this is inadequate, is that already referred to of a lover and his beloved. Lovers rest in one another, not for what they receive, but simply because the beloved other one *is*. They do not beseech each other, or try to change each other's minds. They may indeed use no words whatsoever. They are content to be in each other's presence; to regard each other; to adore; to will perfect love toward each other; to be whole in each other; to murmur sweet nothings!

So you can adore God — through prayers, words, moods, wishes. This does not mean that you have to understand everything God does, nor even like everything. How many lovers understand all the actions of their beloved, or indeed like them?

To adore God is to be content that he is, and so far as may be to rest in him. It is simply to regard him and say perhaps nothing more than: "God." "Love." "Holy." Or to say nothing at all. It is to know that the Love which encompasses the universe, which at its heart always comes forth as sacrificial love outpoured on all creation, encompasses you and dwells in your heart. It is utter holiness. And your adoring response is, "God, I love you."

The important question, however, to begin with, is not so much, "Do you love God?" as it is, "Do you *want* to love God?" If you *want* to, then you have expressed the deepest utterance of the human heart. This is the response of the adoring heart.

Francis of Assisi is reported to have prayed once, "O God, help me to *want* to love you." If you can make this your prayer, then you have adored him.

"*O God, help me to want to love you." " O God, I love you.*"

The Prayer of Thanksgiving

As the prayer of adoration is to love God for himself, the prayer of thanksgiving is to thank him for what he does. It is to say, "God, I thank you for . . ." This is the second most important prayer a person can make to God.

We have already discussed in Chapter 2 the ways by which the prayer of thankfulness can begin. It is to take all the good

things in your life at this moment for which you know you are
not responsible, and to thank God for them.

Your attention then is directed away from yourself — your
needs, your problems, your sins, and all the rest which is *you* —
and outward toward God. To thank God for his gifts is to
break the shell we build around ourselves for protection from
the blows of life. It is to put the stamp of thankfulness upon
our relationship with God because now we concentrate on the
good things that come from a *good* God who loves us.

Furthermore it is by the constant, consistent, day by day,
prayer of joyous thanksgiving that we become joyous and
thankful persons. It is our response to God that determines
the kind of people we become. Hence the importance of
thanksgiving. It is almost as simple as this: What kind of person do you want to become? If a joyful person, then thank
God.

Begin, then, your prayer of thanksgiving by *counting your
blessings*. List them: friends, family, love, health, work to do,
and all the rest. *You* count them . . . You cannot expect too
much from God. You cannot trust him too much as the author of everything good in your life. You cannot thank him
too often for the lowliest of blessings.

Your next step forward in thanksgiving is taken by *accepting your adversities*. This is not the place to discuss that most
difficult of all problems, How can a good and loving God permit so much wrong in the world, especially when the suffering seems to happen to the really good people? This problem,
the problem of evil, we shall have to consider later.

In any case, we are here concerned, not with the philosophy
of the problem, but the practicalities. Evil does happen. Adversities do come. When you have done everything in your
power to overcome them and they still remain, what then are
you to do with them?

You are to *accept them,* believing that God has permitted

them to occur so that through them you may turn to him. It is by taking them as from within the providence of God, for purposes which you do not now know, but which you *trust* will bring you closer to God, that you turn them into blessings.

One of the great eighteenth century men of prayer, William Law, once wrote: "If anyone would tell you the shortest, surest way to all happiness and all perfection, he must tell you to make a rule to yourself to thank and praise God for everything that happens to you. For it is certain that whatever seeming calamity happens to you, if you thank and praise God for it, you turn it into a blessing." The true saint, he comments, "is not he who prays most, or fasts most . . . who gives most alms or is most eminent for temperance, . . . or justice; but it is he who is always thankful to God, who wills everything that God wills, who receives everything as an instance of God's goodness, and has a heart always ready to praise God for it."

The key to the prayer of thanksgiving, then, is to be able to take more and more of the events of life — the good and the bad — into oneself as either directly from the hand of God or with God's knowledge. It is to see in everything something of the movement of his Spirit, and to realize that in and through everything, in every single moment of our lives, he wills for us only perfect love and perfect peace and perfect joy. Nothing, therefore, that ever happens to us can be apart from the love he has for us, and which he has shown most fully in that act where evil did its worst — the death of his Son on the cross.

And now two brief words of warning. This does not mean that you thank God for the evil in the world. The college student who began a conference with the prayer, "O God, we thank thee for the sufferings of others . . ." was confused in language if not in thought. You are not to thank God for evil and all that comes in its wake. It *does* mean that that evil which comes to *you* can be received by *you* as coming from within the final loving concern of God for you. This is why he permits it. "It is certain that whatever seeming calamity happens to you, if you thank and praise God for it, you turn it into a blessing."

Nor are you, because you can accept adversities and turn them into steppingstones toward God, to become complacent about evil. Indeed, you are to contend against evil as strongly as you can, to destroy it however it presents itself to you — in sickness, in social injustice, in discrimination, in poverty, in oppression, or in whatever form — just as God himself contends against evil. You can be counted his friend as you enlist on his side and contend everlastingly against it yourself in your life and in the world around you.

So, then, these two prayers of adoration and thanksgiving are bound very closely together. You thank God for what he does in order to thank him for who he is. And as you love him for himself you see more and more his loving-kindness toward you in all the events of your life.

You can do no better than to begin now with these prayers for which you will find no ending:

O God, I love you

O God, I thank you for . . .

The Prayer of Confession

If you have ever had a disagreement with a friend (or a husband or a wife), you know something about the reason for the prayer of confession. When you have had an argument with someone, you become separated.

This separation will grow worse and worse until somebody says the healing words, "*I am sorry.*" Once these words have been spoken, either aloud or in spirit, separation stops and reconciliation begins. It is the willingness to sacrifice a little bit of ego, to confess that one is wrong, that is the key to a full, loving, creative relationship of friends or lovers restored.

When we begin to recognize God, we recognize that we are separated from him. Indeed, our first awareness of God frequently comes in our realization that we are separated from him and that *we are not meant to be*. Somehow something has gone wrong, and that close friendship or union that lovers intend for each other, and God intends for us with him, has been broken. What is more, we suspect at first and later are convinced that the fault is ours, that we are the ones who have run away from him. He never runs away from us.

And the key to reconciliation with God, as with friend or lover, is, " I am sorry." Then as we turn in honest contrition, we find that he has been waiting eagerly for us. Then he can restore us to the *rightful* relationship he has for us. He is, in fact, even more ready and willing to give us his forgiveness than we are to ask. Indeed, it can be said that he urges and persuades us by every means he can until we finally recognize that we *are* separated from him, that it *is* our fault, and so say, " I am sorry." Then God can begin to have his way with us as love intends.

If you ever as a child disobeyed your parents, suffered in your separation from them in spirit if not in body, then said, " I am sorry," and were welcomed back into the bosom of your family, you know that this " confession " is what your parents wanted. Probably they did all they could to help you, for they wanted you back as a member of the family in good standing. So it is with God. He does all he can through the experiences we have to help us to say, " I am sorry," and rejoices when he welcomes us back into our rightful relationship with him.

We shall, therefore, tell God that we are sorry for whatever we have done that we know we ought not to have done, and for whatever we have not done that we know we ought to have done. This is the general principle, but we must translate it now into practical terms.

There are sins of the flesh and there are sins of the spirit. Although the former are the more obvious, the latter are the more deadly. It is not difficult to recognize the sinful man who eats too much, gets drunk, and commits sexual immoralities. Seldom, however, can we discern within the heart of another all the anger, jealousy, and pride that may lodge there. Even for ourselves we are more aware of the sins of the flesh we commit than we are of the sins of the spirit embedded deep within us.

So there is a popular misconception that the root of sin is man's body and the passions of the flesh. Nothing could be farther from the truth. Man's body is good, because it has been made by God. How is he going to use his body? That is the question. If he uses it only for self-indulgence, that is his sin. If he uses it as the means by which he can best express his love and concern for others, then he has avoided sin. The heart of the matter is his *choice* — whether for himself or for another.

We need to remind ourselves of this distinction between sins of the flesh and of the spirit, because in our attempt to overcome the former we can the more easily succumb to the latter. Suppose you are a person who eats too much. You recognize this sin, confess it, and try to overcome it. You succeed and develop a moderate appetite. Then at a luncheon one day you find yourself seated next to a person who eats as much and more than you did formerly. If you should then say to yourself, "I am a better man than he is because I control my eating," you would become guilty of the sin of pride. This is a spiritual sin and worse than gluttony. Or you may, on the contrary, say as you look at him, "There but for the grace of God am I!" This would be an act of humility and would mark a great advance in spiritual understanding. Should you, however, proceed to think, "How good of me to be so humble!" you would then take pride in your humility and this would be the most deadly spiritual sin of all. This is how closely interwoven are the sins of the flesh and the sins of the spirit.

Even such distinctions as these, however, do not comprehend entirely the question of sin and man's separation from God. To talk of " sin " implies " acts," either committed outwardly or suppressed inwardly. On a deeper level, there is an even more basic separation which colors all the thoughts and actions of a person. He inevitably looks at life from his own point of view. He sees what is good for him. He naturally then tries to make his good *the* good for everyone. In one way or another this is true of all of us. It is this that keeps us from getting closer to God and to one another. And it is the root of the problem.

The trouble is frequently that, although we know this is where the trouble lies, we do not know how we got into this situation. We feel guilty, and yet, however much we search our hearts, can find no reason for this guilt. This is why we can sometimes cry with the psalmist, " Cleanse thou me from *secret* faults, O Lord." Deep down inside we believe that we are responsible for this condition of separation.

It seems that inevitably we are separated from one another and from God. This fact of separation is sometimes called " original sin." It refers to this condition that all men share, which causes them to be biased in their own favor and to choose naturally that which pleases them most, rather than what pleases God or another most. They put themselves, rather than God, at the center of life. And this is the trouble, for from this basic fact of separation arise all our personal sins, whether of the flesh or of the spirit.

Now at the heart of the Christian faith is the knowledge that *this* separation, this basic separation of man from God, has been overcome. God became one with us in the person of his Son, Jesus Christ, who came over to our side as man. Therefore, by our faith in Christ, God has made it possible for us to be right with him. Indeed, even though we may not always *feel* right, the fact of the matter for Christians is that we *are* right — because of what God has done for us in overcoming this separation in Christ.

The fundamental prayer of confession, therefore, is the acknowledgment that we are separated from God, and cannot overcome that separation by ourselves. No amount of effort on our part, no number of good acts, will bring us closer to God. " There is no health in us." To acknowledge this as so and to say, " I am sorry," is to make it possible for us to accept Christ as *the* one who overcomes the separation for us. With this kind of humble confession we can then proceed to thank God for the gift he has given us in his Son, Jesus Christ. Through him we are reconciled to God. We are welcomed as we are accepted and made at one with a forgiving Father.

It is within this kind of framework, then, that we confess our specific sins, whether of the flesh or of the spirit, to God. Although we may indeed tell people whom we have sinned against that we are sorry, the essence of sin is that it is a willful act against God. So, again with the psalmist, we cry, " Against thee, thee only, have I sinned, and done this evil in thy sight." God is sinned against and sees us, even if we harm no one and no one catches us.

We shall confess to God those sins of which we are accused by our conscience. As we draw closer to God, we shall find that our ideas of right and wrong will change. Our conscience will become more sensitive. A man may begin by believing that God wants him only to stop beating his wife (which he does), but he gradually discovers that what God really wants is for him to be concerned above all else to make his wife the happiest person he can. There are, therefore, higher and higher standards of behavior revealed to us as we draw closer to God. And at the same time we see always more clearly how far short we fall of the life God would have for us. This is why a saint, who ascends to the highest levels of personal behavior, has been defined as one who sins less and less and confesses more and more.

As we conclude this section on the prayer of confession, here are three brief points that may help you to avoid unnecessary confusion:

1. *Temptation is not sin.* There is no need to feel guilty because of the temptations that come to you. You live in a world where there are many opportunities presented to you that can lead to sin. Indeed, there are many images and pictures that flash across your mind tempting you, sometimes with no external cause.

There is no sin in the temptations. Sin is in *consenting* to them. Sin has to do with the will. Do you or do you not *will* to commit the sin you are tempted to commit? Only if you will it, consent to it, do you sin.

A modern version of an illustration by William James would describe the relationship between temptation and sin this way (with apologies to William James and all taxi concerns). When you leave a railway train and stand on the platform where the taxis are drawn up, you hear each driver yelling: " Taxi! Taxi! " These are the temptations that come to a man. You are at that moment free of them. Only when you have deliberately chosen one taxi and gone off in it, either to your destination or to your destruction, have you consented to a temptation. It is in the free choice you make of temptation that you sin — not in the temptations themselves.

2. *Private confession is a help to some people.* Private confession takes place when a person tells God, in the presence of a clergyman or priest, what his sins are and that he is sorry for them. He is then assured of God's pardon by the words of absolution of the minister. This is an important means of grace for people who cannot quiet their consciences by confessing alone to God.

The Christian believes that it is God alone who forgives and that he hears the prayers of all those who turn to him in trust and repentance. The fact is, however, that the actual recitation of one's sins before God's duly ordained representative, and hearing the actual words of absolution, brings a sense of forgiveness that is often not otherwise given. It is good for one sometimes to search deliberately for the specific sins to be confessed and then, having mentioned them to God, to hear the words of absolution: " The Almighty and merciful Lord grant you Absolution and Remission of all your sins, true repentance, amendment of life, and the grace and consolation of his Holy Spirit. Amen." " Go in peace, for the Lord hath put away your sins."

The purpose of private confession is to have your sense of guilt removed and help you to capture the joy that comes with a sense of being forgiven. It is of help to some people. If you have a conscience that cannot be quieted no matter how you confess to God, then private confession may be for you a great means of grace. And confession in itself is an act of humility.

3. *Concentrate on Christ — not on yourself.* It is right to be concerned with our sins. It is wrong to be obsessed by them.

Therefore, the best direction for our eyes is outward toward Christ and not inward toward ourselves. If we look at him long enough and seriously enough, he will by his very nature reveal to us the sins he wants us to confess. In his light our sins will be made perfectly apparent to each of us, as he wishes us to know them. It is wholesome occasionally to examine ourselves in his presence. But, having done so with reasonable care, we are not to go on burrowing around in the murky depths of our souls, stirring the waters, fascinated more and more by our search for our sins. Rather, let us lift up our heads and look at him who would draw us to himself. It is in his light that sufficient light is given us to see into the darkness of our hearts.

A traditional devotional exercise that has been of help to

many through the centuries has been to picture Christ on the cross. Then, kneeling before him, you say:

> " O Christ, thou hast died for me.
> What have I done for thee? "

From this kind of relationship will come an inner conviction of the things that you ought to confess.

Thus far we have been concerned with prayers that reflect the most personal conversations between ourselves and God. Now we shall turn our attention to prayers that have to do with our concern for others.

The Prayer of Intercession

This is our prayer for other people. The principle that lies behind praying for others is a very simple one: You are to bring the needs or concerns of people to God and ask him to help them — just as a son would bring the needs of his brothers and sisters to the attention of their father. If it is in accord with his will that those needs be met, then he will answer your prayer.

You will have to be very patient at times. God's eternal point of view is not the same as our impatient point of view. You may have to readjust your ideas as to what the needs are of the people for whom you pray, to make them more in keeping with God's ideas. You can be certain, however, that God wants you to pray for others and that he will, in one way or another, in his own time, and in the *best* way, answer those prayers.

Let us acknowledge at the outset that we are here surrounded by *mystery*. We do not know in every instance precisely how God acts in response to our prayers. Indeed, we do not know why it is that apparently some prayers are answered immediately and just as we hoped they would be, while others seemingly are not answered for years, and then only in ways we did not expect. Some prayers we must in honesty confess do not, to the outward eye, receive any answers at all, or, at the best, very ambiguous ones. There is mystery all through life. We are steeped in it — especially when we wrestle with the mystery of birth and beginning, death and ending, and suffering and sin. We serve no useful purpose by pretending that we see otherwise than through a glass darkly.

At the same time within the mystery that surrounds intercessory prayer, we can also affirm *certainty*. When we pray certain things happen that would not otherwise happen. Perhaps they occur as we expect, perhaps not. But when people pray they have a certainty, on the basis of evidence observed by the outward eye as well as the eye of faith, that things are taking place because of their prayer. William Temple is reported to have said, " When you stop praying, coincidences stop." This is perhaps as good a proof of intercessory prayer as there is. And you can make it yourself. When you pray persistently for a person, see if coincidences do not begin to happen.

When we pray for others, then, we pray with due humility, because we know that we are involved in mystery and do not have all the answers ourselves. We also, however, pray with confidence because of our certainty that God does. So, then, let us turn to consider the best way to pray for people and causes. There are two fundamental principles upon which intercessory prayer is built.

The first is this: *Be expectant, specific, and persistent.* When you pray, expect the very best to happen to the person for whom you pray. Have confidence that only the best will happen, and trust God to bring it to pass. If you are praying, for example, for a sick person to get well, expect with every particle of your mind and will that this is exactly what is going to happen. Picture the person in your imagination as already well, and thank God for already bringing this about. One of the reasons we see so little answered prayer is because we expect to see so little. Actually we can hardly expect too much from God. So when you pray, expect the very best.

Let your prayers be for specific people by name, and for their specific needs. Simply to pray for classes of people, or groups, is as a rule, in personal prayer, totally inadequate. Better to pray for a single person in a personal manner, than for a whole population impersonally. And do not hesitate to pray for what you believe they need. To be sure, you may discover in time that their actual needs are different from their apparent ones, and your understanding will change and deepen. A vague and general prayer, however, is unsubstantial, and it is far more helpful to be concrete and pray specifically for healing, a job, reconciliation, money, or whatever you think the particular need to be.

To be persistent in prayer is to be patient, on the one hand, and to claim from God that which we as Christian people have a right to expect on the other. God's eternity is not the same as our time, and we sometimes become impatient and give up because he apparently works so slowly. We can remind ourselves, therefore, that his grace has all eternity to work in and that our prayers will always be answered — even if it be on the other side of the grave. Even in the short space of time given us on this side, our patient, persistent prayers are prayers of power and bring forth more fruit than the impetuous prayer of a man easily discouraged.

More than this, however, let us not forget that as God's children there are certain things we have a right to expect from him. He has made promises about our never being forsaken by him, about being forgiven, about our never being afraid or alone. He has adopted us through Christ as his children. He has promised us the comfort and power of his

Spirit. All that a human father would do for his children God will do for us — and more. We have a right, therefore, to insist on these promises and to pray persistently for his children whose needs we know and whom we bring before him. And if he seems to pay no attention, it may be (as it often is) that only to our persistent prayer will he reply.

Along with this first principle of intercessory prayer there goes hand in hand the second: *the best prayer is Christ's prayer: " Thy will be done."* This was the prayer he offered to God in the Garden of Gethsemane on the night in which he was betrayed. He asked God very specifically that the suffering he saw before him the next day be taken away. Suffering was not what *he* wanted. Yet he knew that what *God* wanted would in the long run be best for his work, for the world, and for himself. Therefore, he concluded his prayer: " Thy will be done."

It is this prayer of Christ's that makes intercessory prayer Christian prayer. When all our prayers are finally rooted in our desire to have God's will done in those for whom we pray, then we are praying in Christ's name. *These prayers are always answered.* They may not be answered in our way. We may not understand how they should be answered. Sooner or later we discover that suffering is embedded in the very heart of the universe. It cannot easily be avoided. There is no magic word that will turn it aside. Indeed, sometimes there is no way by which God's will can be done except through suffering. Given the world we live in, with the power of man's sin, we cannot escape the suffering that follows. When we look deeply into the mystery of prayer for others, therefore, we are not surprised to see that at the heart of the mystery there is the cross. Christ's prayer that God's will be done was answered in and through his suffering. He who was without sin suffered for all others. This was intercession at its height. God's will was accomplished only by such intercession. It meant suffering. But it was God's way. And it was the best way.

So for us intercessory prayer that is based finally on the prayer that God's will be done may indeed include suffering. This is often God's way. Such prayers for others that are based on Christ's prayer then will be answered always in the best way, for this is God's way. It is the way of the cross.

We can best conclude this section on prayer for others by remembering that we are talking to One who loves those for whom we pray even more than we love them. He is infinitely wiser than we, and will do for them far greater things than we can ever pray for. He has the will and the power, no matter how dark and hopeless the situation may appear to us, to do what is best. Though there is mystery around us, we have the certainty that at the heart of the mystery is the love of God and that he will do for all his children all that a father would do — and infinitely more.

The Prayer of Petition

This is prayer for ourselves. We are meant to petition God for our needs as well as for the needs of others. All that has been said about intercessory prayer, therefore, can also be said about petitionary prayer. Indeed, prayer for ourselves is but an extension of our prayer for others and the same principles underlie both.

It may be worth-while, however, to remind ourselves that we usually begin by asking God to help us in very specific and concrete ways. We want him quite naturally to meet our needs as we see them. So we tell him of our need for a better job or more money or deeper understanding from loved ones or help to get out of a difficulty, or whatever we believe our need to be. It is right to begin by asking God to help us in any way we see fit.

We end, however, by asking God to help us as *he* sees fit,

and to meet our needs, not as we see them, but as he sees them. Our perfect prayer for ourselves as for others is Christ's prayer: "Not my will, but thine, be done." As this actually meant the cross for him, so may it also be for us the only way by which God's will can be done in us.

We shall not be surprised, then, to discover that our prayers are not answered precisely as we would have them. We shall be prepared for a denial of our terms in order that we may come to understand God's terms. His wise refusals of what we want will help us to know what he wants; and when we honestly have come to want for ourselves what he wants, we have attained the heights of petitionary prayer. We know this may mean the acceptance rather than the avoidance of suffering, but we shall not be discouraged, for with the acceptance comes the strength always to bear it well. This is the way of the cross.

As we have seen this to be true of our prayers for others, so for ourselves. This is God's way and it is the best way.

Our prayers of petition, then, will always be expectant, open, and confident ones. We shall be surprised at nothing and prepared for anything as God answers our prayers. Confident that his answers are always the best answers, we shall trust him to provide those answers in his own way and in his own time. If his will can be done only through our bearing some suffering, then we shall rejoice as he gives us strength to bear our cross. This is the entrance for us, as for Christ, into the peace that comes from doing God's will. This peace that is ours in doing God's will, whatever it might be, is the perfect answer for us to our prayer of petition. If this is what we ask for, this surely is what is given, for God is as trustworthy to us as any father toward his children — and infinitely more.

These, then, are the five foundation stones of prayer. All that is later built into the life of prayer rests upon these foundation stones. As each one is incorporated into your regular prayers, and *none* omitted, a firm foundation is made certain.

When you begin to pray deliberately and regularly, the sure way to build is to provide first for these five kinds of prayer. They are the five responses you make to the way God has begun to touch you. Indeed, it is actually more correct to say that these are the five ways God responds through you, for it is he who inspires you to pray. Think, then, of your prayers as really God's prayers, of your desire to pray as God already inspiring you, for, as Paul put it, "it is God which worketh in you both to will and to do of his good pleasure."

God is helping you to build as broad and as strong a foundation as possible, then, as you say *slowly:*

" O God, I love you . . ."
" I thank you for . . ."
" I am sorry for . . ."
" Please help . . . Jane . . . John . . ."
" ' Not my will, but thine be done.' "

5

THE HOUSE THAT PRAYER BUILDS

Let us assume now that the ground has been cleared and the foundation stones laid. You have begun to say your prayers regularly and wish to get on with the construction of your house. The house that is built by prayer is your soul. This soul is the total response of your whole personality to God, that which is completely "you" in relation to God. It is constructed by your prayer. This chapter then is about the general structure and design you can expect your house to take as you advance beyond "saying your prayers."

The first comment to make is that many people do not even realize that there is anything more to the life of prayer than saying their prayers. Indeed, some do not advance beyond the stage of memorizing prayers as they once memorized "Now I lay me down to sleep." As a result, they get discouraged when they have said their prayers, perhaps for years. In their boredom with a dull routine they think that there is nothing more, and so give up even saying their prayers. Prayers continue properly to be *said* always, but there is more to prayer than that. There is a most exciting new house to be built on top of the foundation we have laid in the last chapter.

There are three stories in the house that prayer builds. We shall discuss them one at a time, although in practice it is impossible to separate them so sharply — indeed sometimes you cannot separate them at all. The prayers now to be described are different and yet they merge so closely that it is difficult to determine where one leaves off and the other begins. The three kinds of prayer are these:

Prayers that you *think,*
Prayers that you *feel,*
Prayers that you *will.*

We shall look now at each in turn, remembering that all are involved in greater or less degree in every prayer. You cannot *think* a prayer, for example, without *feeling* something because you have *willed* it.

Prayers That You Think

To *think* a prayer is to use your mind and direct it toward God. It is to use your intelligence consciously in God's presence. This is sometimes called meditation. As vocal prayer is saying your prayers, so meditation is *thinking* your prayers. This is to make the fullest possible use of your intellect to understand some part of the truth of God. To worship God fully with your mind is the purpose of prayers that you think.

There is nothing mysterious or difficult about such prayers. If you have ever thought about God at all, you have, in a sense, meditated about him. What is he like? Why did he begin the world? How can a loving God permit such evil to triumph in his world? If you have ever had such thoughts as these, you have meditated.

Thinking one's prayers deliberately, then, is to proceed directly to wrestle with the problem of understanding God's actions as intelligently as possible. It is to recognize that as a man thinks, so he is, and to attempt to " think God's thoughts after him." This means a concentration about some aspect of God, or his activity, until you come to comprehend it and then to appropriate it for yourself by applying it to your life.

You can, for example, in meditating upon the truth that God is Power, think through the act of creation as a continuing, sustaining act on the part of God; relate this to the problem of atomic power, where the secret of energy itself is unlocked; consider how God's power can be used by men to support creation or to destroy it; and end by resolving to use what power you are given for God's creative purposes. Or, you can meditate upon the loveliness of God seen in the beauty of a sunset, with the changing colors forming a canopy over the sky, sheltering and protecting you, and know yourself to rest under the cover of his wing. Or, you can watch the rain sink into the parched earth and think of how this is like God's love poured on us. This is to think a prayer.

Meditations may be made on anything from the heavens above, to fathom their mystery, to the sparrow who falls to the ground, still within God's loving care. When you use your mind to consider God, his relationship to the world of nature and the life of men, you are *thinking* prayers. Whatever subjects, therefore, help you to perceive, apply, and inwardly digest the reasons for the actions of God, are to be welcomed and fed upon. They will not by any means be the same for everyone. A reliable guide is for you to respond in whatever way God seems to be leading you, and to meditate upon any truth that seems to apply to you.

It is no accident, of course, that most people who take meditation seriously are drawn inevitably to the Bible. Since God has shown himself most fully in the history of the Jews over the centuries, and particularly in the life of one, Jesus of Nazareth, it is natural that the subjects for most meditations should come from the Bible. Here is the record of what God did with his people and in his Son. As we stay close to the Bible, we stay close to the source of Christian thought and life.

There is the clear-cut description in the Bible of how God acts. He is one who judges the sin of all men, irrespective of who they are, and he calls all men to deeper understanding of himself, no matter how far advanced they may consider themselves to be. To keep this kind of picture before us by intimate association with the story of God's action, especially in Jesus Christ, reminds us that we are still judged by him, because we are still involved in sin, and that, regardless of the advances we may have made in the spiritual life, we still are falling short of the goal set for us by Christ. Without this kind of objective standard we tend to judge ourselves only by our own values, rather than by his; we tend to sink into a complacency where we try to believe that God is thinking our thoughts after us rather than our thinking his thoughts after him. The straightforward Biblical account of God shown in Jesus Christ is the best protection against our own subjectivism.

If you have ever read any Bible story, tried to figure out what it means, and then applied it to yourself, you have in a general way, already meditated. Countless boys, for example, have read the story of David and Goliath, identified themselves with David, and perhaps been inspired by him to act courageously when faced with a bully at school. If they could relate their courage to God who inspires them, as he inspired David, they would, of course, make an even better meditation.

Our purpose, then, is to be more definite than we usually are in such casual meditations, and to proceed with a system of thinking prayers based on Biblical scenes. The most intimate and personal relationship with God is made possible only by intelligent meditation; indeed, it marks the greatest step forward in the life of prayer. Let us examine a method for the devotional use of the Bible that will enable us intelligently to approach the inner truths of a Biblical scene so that we may appropriate them for ourselves. These are three suggested steps:

To *picture* a Biblical scene,

To *ponder* its meaning,

To *promise* God something as a result.

1. To *picture* an episode or scene from the Bible as vividly as possible is the important first step. Use your intellect and all your senses so that the scene becomes alive and intimate and personal. Picture yourself as present, either as observer or as participant. All the five senses should be employed: hear the shouts, smell the flowers, touch the rough stones, taste the blade of grass, see the joyful or angry faces of those who hear Jesus. When his disciples listen to him, you listen; when they speak, you speak.

Here, for example, is an imaginative description of the scene where Peter meets Jesus for the first time. Imagine that you are Peter, relating this incident many years later to people who never had known Jesus.

" I shall never forget," you say, " the day I threw in my lot with him. I was a fisherman, just an ordinary, common, every-day kind of fisherman, like my father before me. I was un-couth, with my share of sins and perhaps a little bit more. One day my partners, James and John, and I had spent all morning patrolling our nets. Since we hadn't caught even a minnow all night long, we took the nets in and were washing them on some rocks.

" Pretty soon, along the shore of the lake came a crowd of people — forty or fifty of them — with a young man at their head. As they drew near, this young man, I would say in his early thirties, asked if he could sit in my boat while he talked to these people. I said I would be glad to help him. While I held the boat, he got in and sat in the stern. I took up the oars and shoved off a little distance from the shore, and the people gathered on the bank and the rocks in a little semicircle. For about a half hour he talked very simply to them about God, and his Kingdom, and how they might trust God within his Kingdom. I didn't pay very much attention to what he said, but I was struck by the way he talked. He seemed to know what he was talking about; almost as though he had some kind of inside information about God and his Kingdom.

"When he had finished, he gave them a blessing, and as they were walking off he turned to me and said, 'Simon, let's go out and get some fish.' I answered. 'Sorry, Rabbi, but there aren't any today.' 'Well,' he replied, 'let's go see.' So, to humor him more than anything else, I rowed out, tossed over a net, and, much to my surprise, pulled it in full. I dumped it out on the bottom of the boat, and it was flooded with fish flapping around. I then threw over another net, which was so heavy I couldn't even pull it in, so I called for my partners. James and John then came alongside in another boat. I tossed them a line and we all began to pull. The load was so heavy that both boats began to ship water and we began to go under, with fish flapping all around us.

"For some reason I looked at Jesus, who was sitting still in the stern. Suddenly it dawned on me that somehow he must be responsible for this. Before I knew it, I was on my knees before him crying out: 'Lord, go away! I am a sinful man.' He put his hand on my shoulder and called me by name. As I raised my eyes, he looked at me. It was not simply that he looked at me — he looked through me, and beyond me; it was as though Almighty God himself was looking all the way through me and catching me up within his gaze. For the first time in my life I felt that I was known, really known; that I was held and loved. And then he said, 'Don't be afraid.' How often he was to say those words to us in the years that followed. So, we weren't afraid.

"Well, we landed what fish we could, and rowed back to shore. Then Jesus looked at us and said, 'Now you are going to be fishers of men.' And he and I walked along the beach,

James and John behind us; the waves lapped on the shore; and, as we walked along with him, it was as though the waves of eternity were beating upon our feet.

"Never again when I was with him was I really afraid, because I was known, and I was safe forever."

That is to *picture* the scene.

2. The second step is to *ponder* the scene. Bring your mind to bear as strongly as possible on the scene. What does it mean? What do you think about it? What do you think God is trying to do here? What is he trying to say to you?

For example, as you ponder the scene we have already pictured, one thought that may come to you is that just as Jesus walked into the life of Peter, so God seems always to take the initiative in coming into our lives. He always starts the relationship. Then we respond — or do not respond.

We are free to have him sit in our boat — or tell him to get out! He never coerces, but waits upon our willing consent and invitation to welcome him in. So love always comes to us as a gift, which we are free to accept or reject.

Again, ponder what it means really to be known. What did Peter experience by suddenly understanding that he was entirely known? How few people there are who really know us, or want to know us! How difficult for us to enter fully into the heart and mind of anyone else — even those we love most deeply! Yet there is One who sees into the depths of our hearts, who knows all about us, from whom we can hide nothing. How terrifying and yet how wonderful to be known as Jesus knows us!

Think of our fear because the boat sinks. And mixed with fear is our guilt, because, confronted by the holiness of Christ, we see ourselves as we truly are. How wonderful that to be known by Christ is the means by which we can know ourselves!

Or ponder the meaning of "Be not afraid." All our anxiety,

loneliness, and fright wiped away as we know ourselves to be with One who loves us forever and will never leave us alone! Never again is there anything for us to fear.

You may reflect upon the truth that Jesus always comes into our lives in company with other people. We never meet him alone, but always with others. We may first know him as he appears with our parents or church school teachers or friends. Sooner or later, however, we have to come to have dealings with him all alone. We get personal knowledge of him. This usually involves a struggle, for our first impulse is to tell him to go away because we recognize ourselves as sinful. We have to choose him or our sins. Once this has been settled though, and we understand that we are known and forgiven and there is nothing to fear, then we can go on. We go about our daily living in company with others and with Jesus. And we see our responsibility then to carry him into the lives of people, as he once came into our life with others, and so we too, like Peter and James and John, become fishers of men.

Sometimes it helps to dwell imaginatively on what happened in the lives of the characters *before* the scene unfolds. What was Peter like before he met Jesus? How did he as a fisherman spend his free time? What was he thinking of as he was washing his nets on this day? This is to get a running start on the meditation before it actually begins. We are in any case to think, to apply our minds to the subject matter, to *ponder*.

3. The final step is to *promise*. A meditation is not completed until it has resulted in some action. Indeed prayer is not finally prayer until some act is made. Thus the result of the ponderings can be pinned down and made concrete. If prayer does not result in action, and does nothing more than stimulate the mind and excite the emotions, it is not only useless but dangerous. The final step, therefore, is to *promise* to do some-

thing. It should, if possible, always be simple, definite, and practical, and the sooner done the better.

You might promise, for example, something like this: " God, I promise to invite this one person into my life today as Peter welcomed you into his . . . to try to discover and meet what another's deepest needs are . . . to put away this one sin . . . to try to come to know one person better this day . . . to help anyone I know who is afraid . . . to write this lonely person a letter."

Thus with any Biblical scene there are inexhaustible riches for those who will conscientiously try to think their prayers by these three steps: to picture, to ponder, to promise. This is particularly true as you view the scene on the hill of Calvary and think of what God has done through Christ on the cross there. There are many systems of meditation that have been developed, and you should always follow whatever system leads you most easily into natural conversation with God. What has been described here is simply one very easy system that has been of help to many people.

Prayers That You Feel

To *feel* prayers is to involve your emotions in your relationship to God. When you think about God in any way, your emotions are naturally involved. As you remember God's good gifts, you *like* them and *rejoice*. You are *ashamed* of your failures and tell him you are *sorry*. You *thank* him for his help and tell him of your *love*. Fervor of spirit, depth of feeling, and the longings of your heart are part of the flesh and blood of your prayer life.

You are meant to have your emotions aroused, and the warmth of your feeling expressed, as part of your response to God. You are to use your emotions in your prayers just as you use your mind. These are the prayers that bring color and richness, breadth and length, height and depth, to your relationship with God. They also bring power, because emotions, as a driving force in life, are usually even more powerful than intellects.

As you think of God, therefore, and dwell upon any aspect of his truth in himself or his actions, let your feelings follow quite naturally and express themselves as they will. Let the power brought by emotional drives now be added to your brains as you respond more fully to God.

If you are meditating, for example, upon the beauty of God, and take as an illustration the beauty of nature, do not hesitate to pray in some such way as this: " O God, I marvel and rejoice at the colors of the sky, the movement of the seas, the blowing of the wind in the trees, and the voice of the cricket in the field. How wonderful thou art, holding all that is, letting these works of nature bring the beauty of thy nature to me, and helping me to lift my voice because my heart does sing and rejoice in thy created world! "

If your thinking has led you to dwell on the loveliness of Christ, let yourself go and speak thus with him: " O Jesus, who art the Beloved of thy Father and the Beloved of my soul, I long for thee and thy goodness. I lift my heart to thee. I would love thee with the perfect love thou hast for me. Be thou mine, that I may be thine forevermore. O Christ, blessed art thou whom I love and adore! "

The principle is to let your emotions follow your thoughts naturally. Do not try to force your emotions or strain them or make them express what you do not truly feel. As you meditate upon God and his love for you, the inner motions of your heart will become emotions expressed by loving in return. There is, for example, a peace from God which flows over us as we think of him as perfect peace (" thou wilt keep him in perfect peace whose mind is stayed on thee "). We can, however, receive such peaceful emotions only as we deliberately turn our minds to him. Feelings follow thoughts.

And now, curiously enough, an almost imperceptible change
will begin to take place. The change that comes may not be
one that you are aware of at the time, and you may see it only
as you look back. A husband and wife grow in love for each
other through successive stages, but they are aware of them
only in retrospect, as when they declare, after ten years of mar-
riage, " It is a miracle that we ever dared to get married, for
we had then no real idea of what love was like."

The gradual change in your relationship to God (a love relationship) is marked when one day you discover that you are
paying less attention in prayer to formal steps and external
guides. You are less concerned about specific kinds of prayer,
even specific kinds of requests. Rather than wondering how,
when, or where, they will be answered, you are now content
simply to lay them before God, knowing that he will answer in
his way and time as is best for you.

You are more and more content simply to be with him. You
are aware more than before of being *in* him. The tension or
strain of " you " and " God " as two different persons in a
personal relationship is slackened. It now seems more as though
God were more directly all around you, even within you, almost as though he were in you and you in him. There is an
intimacy that you never had before. God is still another person
and always remains so, but now you are more sensitive to him
as spirit dwelling within you and around you.

As you give less attention to the proper rules of prayer, it is
as though God himself becomes more your guide. You now begin to trust him and to follow leadings that seem to come directly from God within you. You are content with few words,
perhaps only single words: " God." " Love." " Blessed Jesus."
" Holy One."

In this kind of prayer you find yourself one day at the Center. The Center seems to have enfolded you, and all mere ex-

ternals have been dropped off and shut away. So the Quakers have the wonderful phrase of " centering down." Here within us (yet also outside us) is the Deep, the Quiet, the Rest of the Spirit of God himself.

Now you do not move. You do not agitate. You simply *are*. And God is holding you in the Quiet and you rest within him as your Center. God *is*. You two in your personal dealings with each other. You feel no need to speak now, nor to listen. You simply are in God and he is in you. You look at, contemplate, rest in each other, love each other. It is love responding to love. This is to be " prayed through." It is as though you were " inspired," " breathed through " by a Spirit that comes from beyond, wells up within you, and carries you in response back to its source. God having found you, and you having responded, he has now brought you into himself—and yet you are still you!

This is something of a glimpse, at its heights, of what heaven must be: you and the whole company of souls with you in such a relation with God and each other. Here is a foretaste of the glory of being caught up, surrounded, and indwelt by the perfect love that is God. The basic reality is God — God loving you and you being loved through by him. There is above and beneath and within nothing but the all-consuming motions of love, loving perfectly and wholly and completely. And yet you remain. You are not consumed. You are still you! In heaven you are loved and able to love finally and fully and forever, for you are now at one with God, and with all others so bound to him. And from time to time we feel heaven about us on earth!

This, however, will pass. Such an experience of ecstasy is not expected to remain. It may indeed come and go in a flash. You return then to your regular prayers, not impatient because these feelings have gone, but thankful that they have come and confident that they will, in God's good time, return.

The *feelings* will come and go — do not trust the feelings. God remains and you remain — trust him.

Prayers That You Will

To *will* a prayer is to direct your will to God, irrespective of your feelings. It is the final and most essential prayer in the sense that this is " you " praying — the real you as your emotions are not " you." When you have said to God, "I will this . . . or this . . . to thank you . . . or to love you . . . or to have you," you have expressed the very heart of your relationship to God. This will is the core of your soul.

As we have seen, you are to trust, not your feelings about God, but God himself. Whether you feel God near or far away has nothing to do with the fact of God and his nearness to you. The fact is, whatever your feelings, that God is where you are.

So let here a negative word be said about feelings. Important as the emotions are for action — indeed they provide the driving power for most action — they are nonetheless very unreliable *guides* for action. The surer guides are always your intellect and your will.

It is treacherous to count upon your feelings. You may, for example, one day feel happy and the next day feel unhappy for no apparent reason, when your actual condition has not changed at all. You are drawn to like some people and dislike others — again for the most superficial reasons. Sometimes you like the people you ought to dislike and dislike those you have good reason to like. We are all subject to moods and changes of temperament in varying degree, and emotional feelings have frequently no rational rhyme nor reason in their fluctuations.

And so with our feelings about God. Sometimes we say that we " feel close to God." Other times we " feel apart from God." Still again, " we feel God does not exist." These feelings, of course, have *nothing* to do with the matter. God either is or he is not. If he is, he is where you are — precisely there. Whether you "feel" he is there or not has no bearing whatsoever on his actually being there.

So do not trust your feelings as guides in your relationship with God. They come and go. They are helpful when they make you "feel" near him. But nothing has actually changed when those feelings change. God is still there. And so are you.

And the only question is, Do you *want* him there? This has to do with your will. It has to do with your choices. It has to do with your most basic decisions in life. It has to do with the real *you*.

Thus the prayers that mean the most are the prayers that you will. This is not to say that prayers *thought* and prayers *felt* are not honest prayers. It is simply to say that when they are *willed* they are complete.

As a matter of fact, when feelings are withdrawn and you have nothing to go ahead on except your intellect and your will, you can make the greatest forward strides in prayer. It is then that you are able to decide whether you want God for himself or only for his gifts. In a sense it is a great act of trust that God makes toward us when he takes all feelings away to enable us to trust him alone, rather than to trust our feelings about him. This opportunity to *trust* him alone because we know we *want* him alone is a great means of grace which he gives us. So, when your feelings toward God go away, thank God with your will, because it means that you have advanced enough for him to trust you.

To be able to say, "O God I want *you*," is the great prayer of the will. Here you pray to God and hold on to the personal relationship with him, not because you need to, nor because you ought to, but simply because you want to. It is you and God alone in the essential parts of your natures — your wills. And if you cannot say that, perhaps you can pray, "O God I *want to want you*." That is enough.

The house that prayer builds, then, is the house of your soul. The prayer that builds this house is always threefold: thinking, feeling, and willing. Although we have separated them artificially into three distinct prayers, it is clear that they all are closely intertwined. While one aspect rather than another will be stressed from prayer to prayer, all elements are in each, and the most complete prayer includes all equally. The heart of prayer, however, is the prayer of the will directed to the God one *knows* to be true.

So the house is built. The foundation stones are firmly in place and made more secure day by day as your prayers of adoration, thanksgiving, confession, intercession, and petition continue to be said. The dwelling place of the soul is then constructed, with variations for individual patterns, as prayers that stress the intellect take an increasingly important place. These prayers of meditation are the key prayers. The structure is completed as prayers that include your emotions and prayers that are based on your will then take their proper places. This is the mansion where the soul dwells and where God is your constant Companion and Guest.

This is the house that prayer builds. It is a work that goes on as long as we live. Once the house is built, then comes the next step of moving in and making the house a home to live in. It is to this enrichment and deepening of the life of prayer that we now turn.

CHAPTER

6

PROGRESS IN PRAYER

Not to advance in the spiritual life is to go back. As we
grow in age we are meant to grow in grace. But progress in
prayer is never automatic. It comes about only as we deliberately pay attention to God and to developing those habits of
thought and action which keep him before our minds. So we
are concerned in this chapter to consider ways that will help us
more easily to pay attention to him and thus come to know and
love him more.

"Practicing the Presence of God"

"Prayer for busy people" is the concern of this section. If
you are a very busy person, involved in all the demands and
distractions of earning a living or keeping house, so that you
have only limited time for devotional practices, how are you
going to gain the sense of God's presence which is necessary
for progress in prayer?

The secret is to pray in and through all your busyness and
activities. Let the work you do and the people you meet be
themselves the vehicles for your prayers. Try to cultivate the
sense of God's presence, not as something to be gained apart
from your daily living, but as a part of all the events and activities of the day.

Take, for example, *any given moment* on any given day. That moment, and all that is involved in it for good or for evil, is the means by which God is trying to break into your life to communicate with you. No matter what your circumstances at that moment may be, he is as involved in them as you are, and moreover is trying to use them to say something to you. If you are discouraged, he is concerned to give you hope; if you are guilty, he is asking you to say you are sorry, so that you may be forgiven; if you are frightened, he is telling you to trust in him; if you have a task, he offers you the strength to accomplish it. Whatever the conditions of a given moment may be, they are the means by which God comes into your life, so that you may know him better, love him more, and serve him more ably. There is *never* any moment that takes place outside God's providence. So you can be aware of him and respond to him moment by moment in your busyness, and still go about the tasks of the day.

Another way by which you may be helped to practice the presence of God in your daily living is to try to see him in and through the *people you meet*. It is possible to cultivate this practice so that you come to see each person as somehow bearing God to you. You may see this most easily to be true of the people who need you: the sick, the unhappy, the forlorn, the lonely, the poor, the rejected. It is just as true of those who apparently do not need you, and especially of those who do not like you. So when a person comes into your life you can properly ask God, " What are you trying to say to me through this person? " When a person irritates you, God may be saying, " Be patient." When someone criticizes you, God may be saying, " Think of how he could judge you if he knew you as I know you." When you are betrayed by someone you trusted, God may be saying, " Your final trust and confidence must be in me and not in men."

So your response to the person will also be your response to

God. In this way not only will you remain open to every human relationship, and be helped to treat each person as a bearer of God to you, but God will himself come to you intimately and directly and personally in and through all these relationships. He will be as involved in your life as every person is involved. No matter how busy you may be with people, God will be brought to you through all of them, and you will be given a more constant sense of his presence.

Another way by which God's presence may be experienced is by being sensitive to his handiwork and reality in *the world of nature*. The heavens, flowers, birds, mountains, floods, mists, meadows, sunsets, and storms all contain signs and symbols that the whole realm of nature is his. They point to him. It is frequently in this natural world that men and women are first made aware of "something more" than meets the eye, of "something other" brooding over them, of "someone else" beckoning to them, calling them onward. In a moment, perhaps, they are broken in upon, touched, and lifted into another presence. They are in touch with the reality that sustains and lies behind the world of nature, God.

Such intimations as these which seem to come from another world are to be welcomed. You can cultivate sensitivity to these "breakings through" and put yourself in the way of them. Wherever you seem closest to God through the beauty and awesomeness of nature is the place where you can properly go time and again to sense his presence: walking along the beach at the breaking of the waves; at dusk as shadows lengthen and the world for a moment seems to stand still; beneath the stars at night; lying on the bow of a boat as it rides into the rolling sea; inhaling the fragrance of an herb garden; watching a bird light on a branch and fly off instantly. To respond by the lifting of your heart in thanksgiving to God is to be stirred by his Spirit and to be reminded that you are constantly in his presence.

These experiences in nature are frequently the ways by which people are first touched by God. It is as they respond to him in such experiences that they then come to understand that he is infinitely more than an emotional experience related to beauty and wonder, that he is finally the One shown fully in Jesus Christ. This complete revelation, however, comes only as people respond to their best understanding of him where they begin. The God revealed in nature is not the fullest expression of God for the Christian, but he is nevertheless the same God, and it is in nature that he is often first, if imperfectly, known. Once you have responded to the leadings of God and been brought to his deepest manifestation in Jesus Christ, you are then able to turn back to the world of nature and see signs of God everywhere. Having known God's love in Christ, you are free to find and be fed by lesser manifestations of that same love in the beauty of nature. It is a sure sign of spiritual depth to be able to see the glory of God in a rose, for example, and to praise him for it, because you have seen it most fully on the cross.

You may develop a sense of God's presence, finally, by reminding yourself that *God lives within you.* There is the testimony of the " inner light " and the sound of the " still, small voice." Christ is known within, and the interior life can be built upon a quiet and constant inner conversation with him.

A man tells of going into a church late one afternoon. Kneeling down in the shadows there, withdrawn from the busy world, with only the quiet coming and going of others who, like him, had come to pray briefly, he was given a sense of the presence of Christ within him.

" I was gradually aware," he said, " of a presence around the altar which could not be described in terms other than those familiar, though to that moment misunderstood, words: ' Real Presence.' I thought to myself, ' Christ is there.' Then my eyes fell upon a crucifix attached to the wall and I thought, ' Christ is there too.' The people praying next impressed me, and it came to me, 'Christ is within them as well.' Immediately I was overwhelmed by the succeeding thought, 'Why, Christ is inside my own heart.' 'Certainly,' I said, 'Well, speak to him then,' came the thought. So I cautiously asked, 'Why don't you give me more help, Jesus?' 'I will, when you give yourself *wholly* to me,' immediately came the reply. 'All right. Right now I give myself and all I hope to be to you.' 'Then remember I am your friend. I am within you. I will be with you with power forever.'" This is to know Christ within, and is one way to be helped to practice the presence of God.

To summarize, then, busy people can pray in and through their busy activities as they practice the presence of God. He is present in every moment of your life. He is present in every person who has dealings with you. He reveals himself through nature. He is known as a living presence within you. All these ways together will help you to develop a sense of his presence, and, as you respond to them, there will be no end to the increase of grace given you.

One of the masters in this art of practicing the presence of God was a retired soldier known to the world as Brother Lawrence. Near the end of his life he made this comment: "Were I a preacher, I should, above all things, preach the practice of the presence of God. . . . He requires no great matters of us: a little remembrance of him from time to time, a little adoration; sometimes to pray for his grace, sometimes to offer him your sufferings, and sometimes to return him thanks for the favors he has given you, and still gives you, in the midst of your troubles, and to console yourself with him the oftenest you can. Lift up your heart to him . . . the least little remembrance will always be acceptable to him. You need not cry very loud; he is nearer to us than we are aware of."

As a final hint: memorize some reminders of God. Simple little sentences or prayers said frequently during the course of a day will in time lift your mind constantly to God's presence. The best phrases are those you select yourself to meet your particular need, but some typical ones are these: " Glory be to thee, O Lord . . . Praise be to thee, O Christ . . . Blessed Lord Jesus . . . Lord Jesus Christ have mercy on me, a sinner . . . Thou art my God and I will praise thee; thou art my God, I will exalt thee . . . All things work together for good to them who love thee . . . I can do all things through Christ who strengthens me . . ."

Reading, Prayer Groups, and Retreats

These are three aids to progress in the life of devotion which Christians in varying degree have found indispensable. They provide an undergirding and strengthening of the interior life, and in one way or another will make possible an increase of grace for your own life.

Reading. Men and women who have known and loved God in their day have left accounts of their experiences to help us to know and love him in our day. One of the great aids to progress in prayer, therefore, is the reading and inwardly digesting of the experiences of those who have walked with God. Although the forms of expression may differ from generation to generation, the knowledge and the love are the same, offered to God by men of every age.

The book, of course is the Bible. As no other book, this one has led men and women through the ages to feed upon the living Word of God, to be sustained and comforted and guided by him. With the aid of a commentary, such as *A New Commentary,* by Gore (The Macmillan Company), or *Dictionary of the Bible,* by Hastings (Charles Scribner's Sons), for intelligent reading, there is no substitute for the daily devotional reading of the Bible.

Next to the Bible, and also in a class by itself, is *The Imita-*

tion of Christ, perhaps the best loved and most widely read devotional book of the Christian ages (Everyman's Library, Dutton, 1928). A fourteenth century work, probably by a member
of a religious community in Holland, it is made up of a series
of dialogues with Christ, maxims, and prayers. It has an as-
cetic note, not entirely congenial to our modern temper, and
perhaps for that reason all the more important for us to heed.

Then there are certain books of devotion that have earned
the right to be called classics: *The Confessions of Saint Augustine* (The Westminster Press, 1955, or Everyman's Library,
E. P. Dutton & Co., Inc.), the spiritual autobiography of one
of the greatest Christians; *The Practice of the Presence of God,*
by Brother Lawrence (Fleming H. Revell Company, or Forward Movement Publications), in which a single-minded
monk gives simple directions for discovering the sense of im-
mediacy of God; *An Introduction to the Devout Life,* by Francis de Sales (The Peter Reilly Co., Philadelphia, 1942), perhaps the most helpful guide to the life of devotion for busy
people who must live in the world and accept responsibilities
within it; and *On the Love of God,* by Saint Bernard (A. R.
Mowbray & Company, Ltd., and Morehouse-Goreham Co.,
Inc., 1950), which sets forth a traditional pattern for the life of
prayer, especially for those whose main work is prayer.

Other writings have come down through the ages and have
been read and loved by Christians of successive generations.
Any list would include the following:

Andrewes, Lancelot, *The Private Devotions of Lancelot
Andrewes* (Abingdon Press, 1950)

Bunyan, John, *Grace Abounding to the Chief of Sinners*
(Student Christian Movement Press, Ltd., 1955)

Fénelon, François, *Spiritual Letters* (Idlewild Press, 1945)

—— *Letters and Reflections* (The World Publishing Co.,
1955)

—— *Christian Perfection* (Harper & Brothers, 1947)

Fox, George, *Journal* (Everyman's Library, 754, E. P. Dutton & Co., Inc., 1948)

Law, William, *A Serious Call to a Devout and Holy Life* (The Westminster Press, 1955)

Loyola, Ignatius, *The Spiritual Exercises* (The Newman Press, 1949)

Pascal, Blaise, *Pensées* (Everyman's Library, 874, E. P. Dutton & Co., Inc.)

Wesley, John, *Journal* (Student Christian Movement Press, Ltd., 1955)

Woolman, John, *Journal* (Everyman's Library, E. P. Dutton & Co., Inc.)

In the twentieth century as well, spiritual books have been written which promise to meet the test of time as they meet the needs of our generation. They would include:

Baillie, John, *A Diary of Private Prayer* (Charles Scribner's Sons, 1955)

von Hügel, Friedrich, *Letters to a Niece* (J. M. Dent & Sons, Ltd., 1929) and in an abbreviated edition (Henry Regnery Company, 1955)

—— *The Life of Prayer* (E. P. Dutton & Co., Inc., 1929)

Kelley, Thomas R., *A Testament of Devotion* (Harper & Brothers, 1941)

Underhill, Evelyn, *Concerning the Inner Life* (E. P. Dutton & Co., Inc., 1926)

—— *The Spiritual Life* (Harper & Brothers, Little Gold-Jacketed Series)

—— *Letters* (Longmans, Green & Co., Inc., 1943)

—— *Collected Papers* (Longmans, Green & Co., Inc., 1946)

These are simply some of the writings of the companions of the Spirit whom God has raised up to help us on our way.

There are many others. As you begin to read in this field, you will come upon particular authors who seem to write especially for you and your condition. When you find such a one, settle down to make him a constant companion and let him lead you through his own experiences into deeper and richer experiences of your own of the knowledge and love of God.

One final word should be said about spiritual reading: read *slowly*. The material can be taken into your soul only as you "read, mark, learn, and inwardly digest" it. This means little bites at a time, not entire meals. This is why spiritual reading makes such good bedtime reading. Only a few pages at a time are enough. But taken regularly over the years they make possible a great increase in grace and strengthening of the inner life of the Spirit.

Prayer groups testify in the devotional life to the universal human experience that in union there is strength, that when barriers are broken down power is released, and that in relationships between people there are resources for living that a solitary person does not possess. When people pray together, therefore, they are given insights into the power of prayer that they do not receive alone.

A prayer group is nothing more than two or three, or ten or twelve, persons who come together at regular intervals to pray. There is a sharing process that takes place, and friendships are formed as people share their knowledge of God. There is a moving of God's Spirit within a group of people who trust one another as they are led to successively deeper levels of understanding and love of each other and of him.

Prayer groups may exist for many different purposes and center around different concerns. Some, for example, may meet for the specific purpose of praying for others: the sick, those in special need, communities, statesmen, missions, world peace, racial justice, or any other particular cause. Bible study groups, begun and continued in the spirit of prayer, help people to relate the meaning of the Bible to their lives and their communities. Other groups may meet for the study of devotional classics or theological books, or even for the simple sharing of religious experience.

Of whatever nature they may be, prayer groups are at their best when there is a minimum of organization, when no one person dominates, and when each one feels free to bring his own contribution of prayer and concern to the whole group. If you are one person alone and believe that you should belong to a prayer group, the way to begin is to pray. Your prayer may be answered in a day or a year, but it will be answered. Sooner or later you will be led to someone or someone will be led to you. Then you have a group to begin. The way *not* to begin a prayer group is to set about organizing one. The only way is to pray. Then God will organize one for you.

We may remind ourselves that the most natural prayer group is the family group. God has already placed most of us in families, and it is in and through these family relationships that he communicates most frequently with us. It is here that we generally come most naturally first to be aware of him and then to respond to him. It is not simply that "families that pray together stay together," but that in their praying they grow also toward God. Family prayer can make a most important contribution to the personal spiritual growth of each member of the family.

Such prayer properly begins with husband and wife, responding to God and relating their lives to him even before there are any children. Simple grace at meals is perhaps the easiest way to start, for it provides an opportunity to thank God for his gifts. The most natural next step is for the couple to take time in the evening to thank God for each other. This does not have to be done formally. It is enough that time is shared for personal devotions, and that each realizes that he or she is being remembered before God by the other one, and their common life prayed for.

A simple form used by many couples for ten minutes at the end of the day is to have one of them read a selection from the New Testament, followed perhaps by a passage or prayers read aloud from a favorite book of devotion. They then say the Lord's Prayer together and conclude with each saying silently his own personal prayers. The most suitable pattern for each couple will be discovered by them gradually, once they have made the basic decision that, since God has done so much for them, they are going to take some regular time to relate their love and life together to him.

This kind of relationship then sets the framework for family worship as children begin to take their places. Parents will not only see that their small children have a regular time for prayers, and learn such traditional ones as " Now I lay me down to sleep, I pray the Lord my soul to keep," but will want them to participate in family prayer as they grow older. Even quite small children can take their turns in saying grace when the family have meals together. At other times the Bible can be read, thanks given to God for particular blessings given to individual members of the family, and prayers said for special family needs.

Only two things are needed by parents for family worship to be significant: a desire to pray in this way, and a sense of humor. Family prayer is a time when parental reins of authority should be held very loosely and children given their heads as much as possible. In many instances parents will discover that on the way to God they will be led by their little children. And it will not be a formal way. The gift of humor is related to the gift of faith, and a family that can combine laughter and prayer is close to the Kingdom of God.

Retreats are times of rest and refreshment away from the place where you normally carry on your daily activities. They are periods of two or three days, or longer, when people withdraw for quiet, meditation, and prayer, to think through before God the direction of their lives, to regroup their forces, and then to return refreshed and with new perspective to the battle lines of their lives.

A retreat is normally conducted for a group of six to eighteen or more people who gather together either in a retreat house established for such a purpose, or in a conference center which can be adapted for this use. Retreats are arranged either by some sponsoring group or by the center itself. Whatever the nature of the retreat, it provides an opportunity for physical and psychological rest. For the space of time of the retreat you are free from all the daily pressures of living and can begin to slow down your pace.

Primarily, of course, a retreat is a time for more individual attention to be given to God than is usually possible in a busy life. It is taking time out to take stock. The traditional and most effective retreat is one where silence is observed. In the quiet, where no one breaks in upon your thoughts with trivial comment, it is possible to come to grips with the deep things of God known only in the interior life. With the stilling of other voices, the voice of God can more readily be heard. Usually a retreat conductor provides meditations and conducts services which provide a framework for your thoughts and for the guidance of God's Spirit. Otherwise you are alone, yet in the company of like-minded companions, with your thoughts, your reading, your prayers — and your God.

In such a retreat, away from all the petty details of an over-busy life, it is possible to be given something of the eternal perspective upon your life. Here help is given to distinguish again between the important and the unimportant, the right and the wrong, the good and the evil. Visions that have not been seen for a long time can be brought into focus again; broken hopes can be restored, new strength gained, and a fresh confidence in God and his power for your life given. It is then that you return to your daily life where God has placed you, restored and reinvigorated to meet the demands life lays upon you.

A retreat means physical, psychological, and spiritual refreshment. If you have never made a retreat, this may be the time to ask yourself if God is not now placing the opportunity before you as never before: to make a retreat, to be *still* and know that he is God.

A Rule of Life

The world is very much with us. The world is very strong. It is too strong for us and will engulf us if we are content simply to drift. Our life of prayer will soon disappear if we believe it will take care of itself naturally. The best guarantee that we shall not be engulfed by the world is by the adoption of what is called a rule of life.

A rule of life is simply what the phrase implies: a deliberate attempt to conduct our life according to a chosen standard. The adoption of a rule of life is the declaration of our belief that prayer and personal religion will be developed only as we regularly and devotedly pay attention to them. It is to exercise consistently those parts of our life that have to do with our inner relation to God. This is to recognize that prayer, simply when we feel like praying or "when the spirit moves us," is never enough to build on, and that progress is never made when all is left to chance or our emotions. A rule of life affirms that, once having decided what is everlastingly true concerning our devotional life, we then commit ourselves to the best way we know of getting there and abide by the rule as well as we can, come what may.

A rule of life brings stability to the inner life. When we live by some rule, we are relieved of the extremes to which many people go: one day praying fervently and enthusiastically, and the next day suspecting that there is no God and wondering if they did not make fools of themselves the previous day. With a rule, this is settled once and for all. The emotional fluctuations are avoided because our guides are no longer our emotions. When we *feel* apart from God we nevertheless quietly continue to pray because we *know* such moods will pass. Our trust is not in them, but in God. During the times when he seems far away we simply stay with our rule, undisturbed by passing moods.

As you begin to make a rule of life for yourself, there is one word of caution that should be spoken. It is this: *begin with a very simple, easy rule.* The temptation of beginners, particularly in the first flush of enthusiasm, is to try to take huge strides toward God. They usually tire, however, soon become discouraged, and frequently give up the journey altogether. Instead, begin with small, easy steps that you are sure you can take. Then in time, when you are steady on your feet, enlarge your stride. It is much better to begin with a five-minute rule of prayer every day and to stick to it than to start with fifteen minutes that you keep only every other day.

Inexperienced amateurs climbing a mountain tend to exhaust themselves in the first hours as they hurry with long strides up the mountain. Experienced mountaineers, on the other hand, go up the first slopes with short, easy steps — but they keep on going. Make your first rule of life a short, simple one. Then after a month or six months, re-examine it and, if you believe it right, strengthen it. Through the years, with your rule made over, perhaps once a year, as your muscles grow stronger through experience, your progress will be steady, secure, and certain.

The one who can best tell you what your rule should be is God. If you pray quietly and consistently to him about a rule, you will come to an inward conviction as to what it should be. A very simple rule to begin with would be this:

1. To pray for five minutes every morning and every evening, using the " five foundation stones " as a guide.

2. To meditate on some passage in the Bible fifteen minutes a week.

3. To do some kind of spiritual reading at least once a week.

4. To worship God every Sunday, and to participate in at least one other way in the life of your church.

Many people who begin are doing something like this off and on anyway. The value of the rule is to make it precise and definite, so that with this as a starting place they can then progress in a steady direction.

Once the relationship with God is firmly fixed, you can then in response to God be led into the next steps to take. They will always be larger steps — but only gradually so.

When a rule of life has been made, it should — like all good rules — be observed. This is now simply the standard by which you determine to conduct your religious life. It represents a promise made to God that your life will be directed in this fashion. It serves as a rudder to provide your devotional life with purpose and direction. The winds and waves of life which beat upon all of us are so strong that without some rule we are finally engulfed by the world. A rule of life helps to make this impossible.

On Beginning Again

Now anyone who has ever made any promise knows how easy it is not to keep it. Anyone who has ever made a rule of life knows how easy it is to break it! Prayers promised are forgotten and the rule is broken. What then?

When you have broken your rule when you could have kept it (obviously there are times when it is broken unavoidably), the only thing to do is to say to God, " I'm sorry," and *begin again*. There is no need to grieve over it, to brood about it

nor, once we have confessed, to feel guilty about it. This is obviously what happens to any rule (or any act for that matter)
when we depend simply upon ourselves to carry it out: we always fail. This is what we can expect. So, we tell God we are
sorry and begin again, asking him for his help that we may
now keep the rule properly.

The key is in beginning again. Indeed, it can be said from
one point of view that that is what the Christian life is all
about: *it is being willing to begin again.* So often we respond
to God out of some deep experience and promise to lead a new
life with his help. Then we forget his help and fail. This is the
crucial point. We can give up in despair or we can begin
again. It is the starting afresh patiently and in good cheer and
hope that is the mark of the Christian. One of the helpful defi-
nitions of Christianity is this: *the Christian life is a series of
new beginnings.*

The only sin God cannot deal with is the sin of giving up!
When we throw up our hands (and our faith) in despair and
say, " There is no answer to my problem, God has no power
to help and save, there is no hope for me either in heaven or
on earth," then we have plunged into the sin of despair. To
give up utterly in despair is the sin where we deliberately cut
ourselves off from God. And God can do nothing until once
again we turn to him and cry, " Help me," or, " Forgive me,"
or just simply, " God, I'm here." This is to begin again.

On the other end of the scale, God can do nothing when
we believe we have *all* the answers and have all God's help we
need. This is the sin of self-righteousness and pride. God cannot break through this sin until we finally turn to him and say:
" I am sorry. Forgive me. There is no health in me." Then
we can begin again and enter once more into the joy of an
open, clean relationship with God, knowing ourselves to be
forgiven sinners and, therefore, confidently beginning again a
new life with him.

The sum of the matter then is this: as Christians we acknowledge ourselves frankly for what we are — frail, weak human beings, trying to lead our lives as we believe God wants us to, but falling down periodically and failing frequently in even the simplest of moral acts. The power that tempts us to failure, to sin, and to life away from God is so strong that we deliberately adopt some rule by which we try to direct our lives.

We are not surprised when we fail, nor discouraged, for we know this is what we might expect without God's help, so we simply tell God that we are sorry and as simply begin again. This time perhaps we remain faithful to the rule one day longer and we thank God for the added help he has given us. And we begin the next stage the next day. But whether we succeed for periods or stumble day by day, we always keep our direction toward God by our rule of life. When we succeed, we praise God. When we fail, we tell God that we are sorry. Then we pick ourselves up and begin again.

And always we go on our way rejoicing, and confident, expectant, hopeful, encouraged. No terrors can frighten us, no dangers can destroy us, and no evil can finally harm us. We are pilgrims and we are on our way. So we go on rejoicing in all that God had done for us in the past, confident that as we know him now as our Companion along the way we shall one day see him face to face. We say with Augustine: " Now therefore my brethren, let us sing, not for our delight as we rest, but to cheer us in our labor. As wayfarers are wont to sing, sing, but keep on marching." This is to live as a Christian — beginning each day — again and again and again.

7

MATURE PERSONAL RELIGION: ACTION AND WORSHIP

It has properly been said that a man's best prayer is what he does when he is not praying. Important as his religious activities are, it is in his day by day decisions in all the ordinary experiences of life that his religion is shown. To have a mature personal religion is to recognize that our relationship to God is reflected in and influenced by our *living*.

This means in part that our actions are a *result* of our prayers. If our attention to God does not mean more loving attention to men, then something is seriously wrong with our prayers. The results of our prayers are seen in our lives. It is also true that what we do serves as *preparation* for prayer. We cannot live in sin and expect to live with God. How we spend our time outside of prayer determines whether we return to God in time of prayer closer to him or farther away. The person who draws nearest to God is the one who returns with clean hands and a pure heart.

What we do in our lives, then, is not only both a result of and a preparation for prayer, but it is also the surest indication of the maturity of our religion. The mature man of religion sees that his personal religion is not simply a compartment of life, but is part and parcel of all his life.

Guides for Action

It is well to remind ourselves, then, as we examine guides for our action that God is not especially, or even primarily, interested in our "religious" activities, but in *all* our activities. We show our response to him by our actions throughout the week, as well as on Sundays; in our hours of employment and leisure, as well as in our hours in worship; in the way we treat the members of our family as well as the way we usher in Church. God is just as concerned with how much money we spend on luxuries as with how much money we give in church; with our sex life as with our prayer life; with the control of our temper and talents as with our piety and devotions. There is no area of life that is not part of life under the Lord of all life.

At the very heart of personal religion is our action, how we behave toward others. Although religion is more than morality, if it does not help and guide us in our moral decisions, it is an inadequate and finally harmful religion. Three words that provide some guidance for our actions, and point to principles that help us understand something of how God would have us act are duty, love, and justice. We shall look briefly at each.

To begin with *duty* is simply to comment that our first obligation in life under God is to pay the debts we already owe. The surest guide to the will of God in most experiences is to respond to him by going about our business and carrying out our duties. Each of us is involved in a whole network of relationships which can be maintained and strengthened only as we discharge our obligations.

Indeed, there are many times when all the broken pieces of life are held together only by a sense of duty. It is this that gives a sense of direction and purpose for most of us most of the time. Not only personal relationships, but the structure of society itself is held together as we carry out our duties to one another, as we keep our pledged word — even though it be to our own hurt. This is the first level of all Christian morality.

And the second level is *love:* " thou shalt love . . . thy neighbor as thyself." To love is an act of our will toward the good of someone else. It has nothing essentially to do with whether we like the person or not. Christian love rests upon what we want for our neighbor — his greatest good under God.

The personal relationship that exists between a man and his wife bound together in Christian love is the most obvious illustration of this level. The concern of each is always about *the other one.* There is an outgoing care and direction which can absorb all differences of opinion and emotional upheavals. Each person knows that the most important fact about the relationship is that he is loved by the other one. This knowledge, and the experience of actually being loved, in turn helps him (or her) to love all the more in response. The guide to moral action in personal relationships is always to be concerned to act for the good of the other person.

Society, however, is largely impersonal, and it is simply impossible to enter into personal relationships with many people. A father, for example, may have a relatively clear idea of how he can express his love for his wife and children, perhaps even for his next-door neighbor. But how can he express this same Christian concern in such complex social issues as war and peace, full employment and the guaranteed annual wage, segregation and public housing? Yet he is called upon as a Christian to act as a Christian citizen on just such issues as these.

So, the final guide is *justice.* In all the impersonal relationships of society, the Christian will support those forces which seem to him to promise a more just social order. They may be " Christian " forces or they may not. He will seek to strengthen those parties or causes or groups which, in his best judgment, will make it easier for men to love their neighbors as themselves. He will not be discouraged because the perfect society of perfect love seems far off, but will work for approximate goals, so that in his day he may be a contributing influence toward creating a more just social order. It has been said that justice is love working at long range; impersonal social forces working for justice are the expression of persons motivated by love.

The guides for action, then, for a Christian in his personal as well as impersonal relationships, in all the areas where he is touching the lives of others, arise out of the principles of duty, love, and justice. These provide the framework within which he carries out and reveals the strength and conviction of his personal religion.

Worship as the Central Act

Personal religion also means *worship*. Worship is our central act toward God. It is the corporate activity of the people of God toward God. This action may be one of praise and thanksgiving, of confession, of petition and intercession, of any or all of these elements together. Our mature personal religion involves not only our life of personal prayer, and personal and social action, but also our participation in *corporate* worship. Corporate worship is the action of a people who are bound together in a special relationship to each other and to God.

We considered in Chs. 1 and 2 how the Spirit of God might be thought of as going out into the world touching us in various ways — through nature, our search for truth, beauty, and goodness, our unmet needs. Then, as we respond to the leadings of this Spirit, we are brought closer to an understanding of the meaning of our life under God. But there is always something more than that. As we respond, we are led finally by God's Spirit into that community founded by the Spirit where men know fully who they are because they know fully who God is. We know ourselves to be the children of God, because we know who our Father is. And this community of which we are a part is where Jesus Christ is confessed, adored, and worshiped. The family centers around him. This is the Church.

The " inspirer " of the life and worship is God's Spirit and Christ is the center. Within the family are God's own people. Their purpose as members of his family is to set forth and declare who *all* men are — sons of God, the Father of all men.

This is not the place to describe how all this came to be. It is enough to point out simply that God has always dealt with people in their relationships with one another. He chose the Jewish *people,* made a covenant with them, and spoke to individual members of that people only so the whole people might respond fully and faithfully to him. The story of the Old Testament is the story of how God chose them, led them, delivered them, loved them, pleaded with them to be his people, as he was their God. He had chosen them so that through them he might be known to all men.

When they persistently refused, he sent his Son to establish a new covenant or relationship. It was to settle once and for all the issue between a holy God and the guilt of man. While on earth, Jesus Christ taught and healed and preached. Then, on the cross, on behalf of all men, he offered a full, perfect, and sufficient sacrifice, oblation, and satisfaction for the sins of the whole world. This expression of what God's mind is really like showed how much God loved the world from the very foundation of the world. He loved men so much that only the sacrifice or offering of his Son could show it forth fully and adequately.

This, then, lies at the heart of the mystery of God: *love in action is sacrifice.* The cross on which the body of Christ is broken is the symbol of that which holds and heals the broken relationships between man and God. The cross links man below and God above. It is held together by the offering thereon of the perfect Man and perfect God. So the whole mysterious enterprise of man and his world and his Maker is revealed as built on sacrifice. Sacrifice is as high and deep as eternity, and wholly reveals what God is like in his dealings with us.

Once Jesus had left the sight of men and returned to his Father to intercede continually for them, his Spirit was given to the world. This is the Spirit who has touched men in the many ways we have seen down through the ages. As men have responded, they have been drawn into the family of God's people — the Church.

This is not to say that Christians are, therefore, better people than other people. It is to say that as Christians we know who we are and that we have been chosen to live as members of this family for a purpose: that all men might discover who *they* are too. This is the Church, the family of God's people, bound together through time and space by his Spirit, where his Son Jesus Christ is known and confessed, and whose central act is the worship of God in the name of his Son.

The heart of God's action toward man, then, is sacrifice — as shown on the cross. The heart of man's response to God is also sacrifice — as seen in his worship. The essential nature of the relationship between man and God is love. Love in action always issues in sacrifice. The great act of love of the members of his family toward God is in their worship which is an offering or sacrifice. We offer ourselves and one another in the great prayer of the Church for all men. We join our prayer to the prayers of Jesus Christ who continually intercedes for all men. By virtue of who he is we dare to make our offerings to God and our intercessions for one another and for the world.

Most of all, however, as Christians we present *the offering of Christ himself.* Since worship is essentially an action toward God, inspired by his Spirit, its inner meaning is finally revealed only sacramentally — that is, by an outward and visible sign of an inward and spiritual grace. This is set forth most clearly in that central act of Christian worship — the breaking of bread and the drinking of wine. In this sacramental action the bread and wine signify the body and blood of Christ, and the prayer is offered that as Jesus is remembered and recalled, his Spirit may enable Christians to be made partakers of his body and blood. So we receive him spiritually to the refreshing and strengthening of our souls.

The Christian family in this action sets forth that living sacrifice or offering which was made once and for all on Calvary. This was the great offering of Christ himself for the world. This offering is continually being made by him. Our offering of ourselves, our alms and oblations, bread and wine, is joined to his and *in his name* is wholly acceptable unto God.

This offering of Christ's is the heart of the worship of the Church. As members of the Church, we are incorporated into his eternal offering and, by virtue of that, we make our own offering in our particular time and place. Because the eternal and invisible and spiritual are given outward and visible signs in this act of corporate worship, it is sacramental worship. By participation in this act of worship, and the reception of his body and blood, we are strengthened to become more and more that which we already are, and which was declared by the sacramental action of Baptism: members of Christ, children of God, and inheritors of the Kingdom of Heaven.

The mature life of the Christian, then, is one of love toward man and of love toward God. It is a life of action and a life of worship. Since the action of love always issues in sacrifice, and the heart of worship is sacrificial action, all of life for the Christian is of a piece. Whether it be in our daily activities or the religious activities of our worship in church, our life as a Christian is an offering of love. In response to the great love of God given in Christ, in whom is our hope for eternity, we offer to God and man all that we are and all that we do. Whether we live or die we are the Lord's. And whatever we do, we do it as for him.

There is no reason for a Christian to do anything except for the glory of God. If this is what we want to do in our action and in our worship, then it is to the glory of God. This is the meaning of mature personal religion: " to glorify God, and to enjoy him forever." So let us turn to consider finally that joy which is our intended end.

CHAPTER

8

ON SUFFERING AND JOY

Man was made for joy and woe;
And, when this we rightly know,
Safely through the world we go.

· · · · ·

Joy and woe are woven fine,
A clothing for the soul divine.
— William Blake, " Auguries of Innocence "

At the heart of the Christian life there lies a great mystery:
suffering and joy are inextricably bound together. The ab-
sence of suffering does not bring joy. Indeed, there is no abiding joy except as it rises out of suffering. The path to joy is
discovered as sufferings are accepted for the love of God. The
greatest joy of all for the Christian is to know that as he gladly
embraces his sufferings for the love of God he offers his most
potent prayer to release the power of God in the world.

This does not mean, as we have already seen, that we are
to accept evil or suffering complacently and make no effort to
remove their causes. On the contrary, as Christians, we are to
fight against them unceasingly. Nor is this to say that God
sends suffering to particular persons as punishment for their
sins. It does mean, however, that since sin and suffering, dis-

ease and death, are actually here, God permits them, and we must reckon with them. They then may be the only means whereby we come to know God and experience his joy. As any surgeon does, he allows us to suffer the pain of an operation in order that we may get well.

To see this more clearly we must deal with two questions. The first is, How are we meant to respond to all life that is given us? And the second, How are we to respond in particular to the sufferings that are given, when everything has been done, humanly speaking, to remove them?

The clearest answer to the first question, and one that provides a framework for the second, is essentially a very simple one. It is to recognize that all life is a gift. Life is sheer grace. It all comes from God. As we accept all life from him, and then in our prayers and actions offer it back to him, we begin to share in his divine purpose for ourselves and for the world.

An ancient prayer puts it this way: " Accept, O Lord, my entire liberty, my memory, my understanding, and my will. All that I am and have thou hast given to me; and I give all back to thee to be disposed of according to thy good pleasure. Give me only the comfort of thy presence and the joy of thy love; with these I shall be more than rich and shall desire nothing more."

If this kind of prayer expresses in any way our attitude toward life and God and all that life brings, then we have an undercurrent of zest and excitement, purpose and enjoyment, that will not be destroyed, no matter what comes. This is to say that we are out in the main stream of life and glad to be there, even when the waters are turbulent. We then have a sense of understanding that our life, with all its joys and sorrows, comes from God, that where we are in life is somehow where God wants us to be, and that all we are meant to do is to try as well as we can to respond to him, to offer it all back to him, and to carry on for him and in his Spirit. This is the way by which joy becomes the lasting and enduring experience of all life. It is given as we respond in this way to what life brings, and provides an inner lift of our spirit toward God in and through everything.

This is an attitude that most of us perhaps can readily accept and cultivate when life is going smoothly and presents no great difficulties. It is another matter, however, when things go wrong, when obstacles are placed in our way, and when we have to suffer unexpected and even undeserved hardships. Yet it is here, *especially* here, that the path to joy is discovered. So we turn to the second question, How are we to respond to the sufferings in life that come, when everything has been done to remove them?

The secret is for us to accept such sufferings joyfully for the love of God. This is quite a different thing from gritting our teeth to endure them in a spirit of resignation. For us to accept suffering willingly and gladly is to help Christ to release God's power in the world to fight against the power of evil and sin and suffering. This is to share in a measure the same joy that was set before him, for which he endured the cross.

The most powerful of prayers is to take our sufferings for the love of God, offer them to him, and then carry them as crosses to be borne joyfully for Christ's sake. There is an abiding joy and enduring peace then held out for all of us when we suffer, for this is the way by which we can come to see some purpose and meaning in our sufferings.

This is the kind of prayer we can make when we have had come upon us pain and agony, either physical or mental or spiritual, when we have tried by every human means to combat it and it still remains: "O God, I do not understand why this should happen to me. I know only that it is here. I cannot avoid it. And you permit this now to happen to me, for some purpose which I cannot now discern. I, therefore, in your sight, as honestly as I can, do take it into myself for the sake of

Christ who suffered for me. And now with him I offer it and myself back to you, knowing you will do with it and me whatsoever is right and good. In your good time and in your own way I am confident you will make clear that your way is the best way, and I shall then know the reason why. In the meantime, you will not give me anything to endure without the strength also to bear it. I pray that in my dealings now with others some degree of the fruit of your Spirit may be shown forth to them, and that through me they may be led to thee. Give me, then, your grace for this day, that I may in some measure be gentle, peaceful, joyful, longsuffering, good, meek, temperate, full of faith and love. So I thank you for the trust you now show toward me. I promise to hang on and trust in you alone, come what may; through Jesus Christ my Lord. Amen."

It is not simply that this kind of prayer gives us grace and strength to accept our own sufferings. Though this is true, it is much more than this. Every act of joyful acceptance of our sufferings for the love of God releases a power in the world that helps all men to carry their crosses. Each such act sets free one more channel for the power of God in the lives of men, so that there is released an access of strength for every person who is carrying on his own battle against temptation or sin or suffering. In this way we help to marshal more of the resources of God in his continuing struggle against all that is evil and wrong in the world. Our individual response to him, by embracing our suffering for love of him, makes his Spirit more available for all men in their own individual struggles against evil in their own lives.

There is an interrelatedness of the Spirit in and through all human relationships. Perhaps, when all is said and done, the greatest help we can be to one another is to accept our own suffering joyfully for the love of God and thus release as much of God's power into the world as we can, in order that all men may be strengthened by his Spirit to embrace and carry well their own crosses.

Consider, for example, a middle-aged father who is suddenly struck down with a disease that medical authorities state will be fatal within five years. He has a wife and four children. As news of his illness spreads, former friends from every chapter in his life come to visit him. At the end of a year in bed, where he has waged a consistent and courageous battle, and shown forth nothing but a gracious acceptance of his illness, he can say: " I am not yet precisely sure why this should have happened to me, but already I can say that more good has come out of it than evil. Because of this, every relationship in my life, especially the snarled and broken ones, has been straightened out and healed. Every single one is now full of grace. So no matter what happens in the future, I cannot but thank God for his goodness to me in letting this come to me." This is finding joy through suffering, and has meant that everyone whose life was touched by him has been given power and grace for his own life and struggles.

Mental and spiritual sufferings are sometimes infinitely more difficult to bear than physical pain, yet the same truth of joy found through suffering is discovered there as well. Here is the story of a woman who through the most intense personal suffering was led to the joy of the Christian life, and in the process so touched the lives of many others that they too were encouraged on their way. All that her life meant came to an end when her husband announced one day that he planned to leave her, and proceeded then to divorce her. All that she had lived for, as a wife and the mother of two children, she suddenly discovered was not enough. Although she had no religious faith to begin with, she was helped by Christian friends to see that her first responsibility was not to condemn her husband but to look within her own self to examine how she might have been responsible and to look outside herself to

God for help. After months of interior struggle, she was able to relate herself to God fully and wholly. Soon afterward she found employment, and from her first week's pay check of twenty-five dollars she gave two dollars and fifty cents as a " thank offering to God for being so good to me."

Years later she has now deepened and matured into a woman of profound Christian faith, with an unshakable conviction that " all things work together for good to them that love God," and is a living witness that with Christ one can do all things. She has now become a person to whom others in their sufferings turn for counsel, guidance, and strength. " It is the miracle of God's grace," she writes, " that not until I almost died with pain at what had happened was I able at first barely to get up and stumble on, but then in time to rejoice that this suffering had come to me. This was the gate I had to go through to discover the abiding peace and joy that God holds out for those who trust in him. So now, while I miss my husband, of course, I still can thank God for his great and undeserved goodness to me." So for her also suffering taken and offered back to God was the way to her living joyously and usefully.

The reason that suffering joyfully for the love of God is so powerful is very simply that this is the way of the cross. This is the way Christ did his work. It was not only in his living and teaching and healing, but finally in his dying on the cross, that he was able to accomplish that which he was meant to do in redeeming the world. The world is a different place because he accepted joyfully his sufferings for the love of God.

And it is not too much to say that the world can be a different place as we accept joyfully our sufferings for the love of God. This is to have some part — a small part, but our part — in Christ's great act of redemption. It is to make available for all men our share in his Spirit. There is, therefore, no such thing as " useless " suffering. On the contrary, suffering for

God, in the spirit of Christ, is the most " useful " act a person can do. People who are sufferers permanently are potentially the most useful citizens in God's Kingdom. Every ounce of suffering accepted in this way is transformed by God into power to be released to his glory and for the good of men.

This is the path to joy, for there is no joy greater than knowing that we are partakers with Christ in the work God intended for him and for all the members of his body. This is to serve on earth Him from whom we came, to whom we belong, and with whom we shall live forever. It is for this that we were born.

This joy is not confined to our life on earth. It also is part of life in heaven, and is shared by all those who live with God as they offer him their sacrifice of praise and thanksgiving. The adoration of God by the whole company of heaven is the joyful act by which they help to release for us the power of God's Spirit for our pilgrimage on earth.

There is no sharp division, therefore, between our life as Christians now and our life with God and his people after death, for nothing, not even death, can finally separate us from his love in Christ for us. The essential nature of that life is action for the love of God, and worship in praise of him. This means suffering joyfully for his sake on earth, and it brings with it a foretaste of that perfect joy that shall be ours in heaven. This joy is the love of God in our hearts now and forever.

Whether on earth or in heaven, then, we join our song to the song of the angels and archangels and the whole company of heaven: " Holy, holy, holy, Lord God of Hosts. Heaven and earth are full of Thy glory. Glory be to Thee, O Lord Most High. Amen."

PRAYER AND PERSONAL RELIGION

As Christian men and women living in the rush and roar of modern-day America, we are often criticized for spending too much time going about doing good — and too little time cultivating our inner life through prayer and personal devotions. We believe in prayer — we hear of great and wonderful things being accomplished through its power. We know that prayer has always been a vital factor in the life of every great Christian personality. Furthermore, probably everyone who reads this book has had at least on occasion some meaningful experience of prayer. But when it comes to prayer's actually being a vital, constant, and satisfying part of our day-by-day routine of work, play, and family living, what success can we claim? How can prayer become so important to us that we find ourselves *making* time for it? In short, how does one get from the point of agreeing that prayer is a "good thing" to the point of practicing prayer as a mature Christian? *Prayer and Personal Religion* sets out to help people find some answers to these questions. If you are willing to experiment with the author's step-by-step directions for establishing communication with God, you may be in for some interesting results. You may find yourself impatient at the slow pace he sets for you, frustrated at your own inability to appreciate fully the more mystical experiences he describes, or rebellious at having to admit that it is God and not yourself who decides the final answers to your prayers. But it is well worth a try if you are really searching for a relationship with God that fills your need more adequately than your present prayer habits seem to indicate.

OUTLINE AND DISCUSSION QUESTIONS

Discussion I. Chapters 1; 2; and 3. God has already established a relationship between himself and his people in which he seeks to draw all men to himself. He has taken the first step — made the first advance. Since he knows us better than we know ourselves, he is always willing to accept us as we are and to listen to even our simplest prayers.

A. What are some of the common experiences of life through which you have felt God speaking to you or influencing your life?

1. In the light of the author's description of how God touches the lives of people, can you now identify other experiences of your own as instances of God's breaking through or of your response to him?

2. As you understand the person of God, is he someone to whom you really want to pray as an adult Christian?

B. Do you remember any prayers you used most often as a child? How do they compare with the three "selfish" prayers mentioned by the author?

C. Do you agree with the author that the time and place for prayer are relatively unimportant as long as you find suitable ones and make them habitual?

1. Do you think your reaction might be a purely personal one, since different people react to this suggestion in different ways?

D. What is the basic difficulty in making the prayers found in printed devotional material your own? (Perhaps you might like to bring examples and discuss their usefulness and validity in the light of this discussion.)

Discussion II. Chapter 4. There are five basic kinds of prayer: *adoration* — "O God, I love you"; *thanksgiving*—"I thank you"; *confession*—"I am sorry"; *intercession*—"Please help others"; *petition*—"Please help me."

A. Think of some of the prayers you use most frequently either at home or at church. Into which of these categories do they fall?

B. Which of these kinds of prayer do you pray most often? Which are you most apt to neglect?

C. "Not my will, but thine be done." What are some of the implications of praying this way? If we are honest in this petition, how might it affect our specific requests in prayer?

D. Can you say that God does not answer prayer simply because he does **not** grant your petition in the way you ask it? Do you think that God sometimes answers prayers in ways we do not recognize?

1. Does the act of stating your petition in prayer relieve one of all further responsibility in the matter?

Discussion III. Chapter 5. A regular and meaningful prayer life contributes to the total response of one's whole personality to God. As one advances beyond the simple exercise of "saying one's prayers," he begins to experience prayers that are thought, felt, and willed.

A. What are some of the obstacles in the way of developing a workable system of meditation that meets our needs without becoming a mere ritual? How does one go about removing some of these?

1. Do you find that picturing a scene such as the one in which the author describes Jesus' meeting with Peter is helpful to your personal meditation, or is the fictionalizing of Biblical incidents an obstacle to you?

B. Does the idea of achieving a feeling of intimacy with God appeal to you as something you would like to cultivate? Can you discover why you feel about it as you do?

1. What are some of the dangers of confusing an emotional attitude with a mystical experience?

C. What do you find most difficult to understand in the author's explanation of willed prayers?

Discussion IV. Chapter 6. Since there is no moment of our lives that takes place outside the providence of God, our progress in prayer continues as we learn to cultivate his presence as a part of all the events and activities of our daily living. The Christian needs to adopt a rule of life affirming his constant and regular attention to the matter of prayer.

A. What seems to you to be the biggest stumbling block in the way of actually practicing the presence of God in one's normal daily living?

B. What kind of understanding and acceptance of people does a man need to cultivate if he expects to be able to see God in people?

C. Is the person who prefers to worship God alone on a hillside rather than in church experiencing the presence of God according to your understanding of the author's explanation of finding God in nature?

D. If you have ever been a part of a prayer group or retreat, what problems were most evident in achieving a vital prayer experience? What real values did it contribute to the group members?

Discussion V. Chapters 7 and 8. The mature life of the Christian is one of love toward man and God. All of life is of a piece, since love in action results in sacrifice just as the height of worship is sacrificial action. This kind of life, in which we come to understand that we are partakers with Christ in the work of God, leads to the lasting and enduring experience of joy which knows no limits.

A. How are the three guides to action (duty, love, justice) related to or influenced by one another in practice?

1. Can you agree that the ancient statement, "Love God, and do as you please," is an adequate guide to Christian action?

B. What does the author mean by "The heart of man's response to God is also sacrifice — as seen in his worship"? (Page 87.)

C. What is your understanding of the author's discussion of accepting our suffering gladly? Is there suffering that should not be received gladly?

D. What is the relationship of sin to suffering? of forgiveness to joy?

E. If you were to make your own "rule of life" with regard to prayer and personal religion, how would it compare with the one offered by the author on page 79?

This Guide is set up on the basis of five sessions. However, by combining II and III, and IV and V, eliminating some of the questions dealing with personal experiences, the material could be dealt with in a series of three sessions.

This Study Guide was prepared by Mrs. Marcus J. Priester, curriculum writer,